THE HARROWSMITH COUNTRY LIFE
BAKING BOOK

THE HARROWSMITH COUNTRY LIFE
BAKING BOOK

Edited by Sandra J. Taylor

Camden House Publishing, Inc.
A division of Telemedia Communications (USA) Inc.

Camden House Publishing, Inc.
Ferry Road
Charlotte, Vermont 05445

Library of Congress Cataloging-in-Publication Data

The Harrowsmith country life baking book / edited by Sandra J. Taylor.
p.   cm.
Includes index.
ISBN 0-944475-28-0 : $18.95
1. Baking. 2. Desserts. I. Taylor, Sandra J.
II. Harrowsmith country life. III Title: Baking book.
TX765. H365   1992
641.7'1--dc20   92-12786
                                                     CIP

Design by Eugenie S. Delaney
Front and back covers and inside photographs by Becky Luigart-Stayner
Food styling by Susan Herr
Illustrations by Pamela Carroll

Typesetting by
Fletcher Typesetting
Depot Square
Peterborough, New Hampshire 03458

Trade distribution by
Firefly Books Ltd.
250 Sparks Avenue
Willowdale, Ontario, Canada M2H 2S4

Printed and bound in Canada by
D.W. Friesen & Sons
Altona, Manitoba

Cover recipe: Chiffon Cake, page 32

CONTENTS

——— ❧ ———

INTRODUCTION 6

PIES 10

CAKES 28

COOKIES & BARS 70

MUFFINS 98

BISCUITS, BUNS & ROLLS 116

QUICK BREADS 150

YEAST BREADS 170

INDEX 216

INTRODUCTION

— 🐝 —

During the summers of my childhood, I would divide my time between two sets of grandparents. Mommy, my father's mother, lived in Corpus Christi, Texas; Honey and Grandpa lived in the small southeastern Texas town of Rosenberg, not far from Wharton, where Academy-Award-winning playwright Horton Foote grew up and set so many of his plays and films, including "The Trip to Bountiful" and "Tender Mercies."

Both grandmothers were exceptional bakers—each with her own specialties and style of baking. Honey was a blue-ribbon winner for her breads and rolls—as well as her pickles and other canned goods. When I was old enough to be helpful, I would stand by her side at the round oak table in the kitchen and wait for my turn to contribute to the project at hand. If it was making bread, she would let me punch down the risen dough in the large, earthenware bowl, pushing my small fists into that smooth, cool mass, elbow deep. Then she'd gather up the deflated dough, working her own magic into it, and place it in loaf pans for another rising.

Setting those aside, she would turn next to making cinnamon rolls. I'd watch her deftly knead then gently roll out the plump dough. While she buttered its soft surface, I would mix together the sugar, cinnamon, and raisin filling, carefully sprinkle it on top, and press it lightly into the butter, licking the sweetness off my fingers when I was through. Then she'd roll up the dough, slice it crosswise, and place the pinwheel shapes into pans. These, too, would be allowed to sit until they achieved the proper size.

The most difficult chore of the day, of course, was waiting—for the rising and then the baking, for the tantalizing aroma of yeast breads and sweet rolls would fill the high-ceilinged kitchen and spill out into whatever room I happened to be in, kindling my appetite. When they were done, Honey would turn out the loaves of bread and let the rolls cool in their pans. Meanwhile, she'd combine some confectioners' sugar, chopped pecans, vanilla or almond extract, and either milk, water, or fruit juice, and then pass the mixture to me.

My job would be spreading this sweet, white concoction over the warm cinnamon rolls, making sure to apply the icing evenly and, most important, to leave enough behind in the bowl for myself. Then we'd sample the finished products, slathering butter over thick slices of bread or, as I was inclined to do, pulling out the interior of a cinnamon roll and eating that tender center first, followed by the outer concentric rings. A loaf or two of bread and a pan of rolls would be kept for the following days' use; the others would be sealed in plastic bags and placed in the deep chest freezer that occupied one wall in the kitchen. A similar ritual existed for Honey's kolaches, with their prune or poppy-seed filling, and her feather-light dinner rolls, which have their own nostalgic associations.

Five years ago, when I bought an old Cape Cod house that I'd been renting, my parents were in the process of distributing amongst my sister, brother, and me some of the furniture, dishes, linens, and various other odds and ends from their households as well as from my grandparents'. Being the sentimentalist/ packrat that I am, I asked them to include anything that no one else wanted— those items they might otherwise have thrown out—no matter how ordinary or insignificant they might seem. It took weeks for the moving van to make its way from Texas to New Hampshire, but when it finally did arrive late one August afternoon, I had my work cut out for me, positioning rugs, arranging furniture, unpacking boxes, and deciding how much of the dishware to keep accessible for day-to-day use.

About a year after I received these gifts, I was sent another box of "leftovers," and included with the aprons, assorted mixing bowls, and kitchen utensils was a small, metal 3 x 5 card file. Inside, arranged under food categories from Beverages to Vegetables, were the recipes that my other grandmother, Mommy, had collected over the years. (Today, at age 96, she no longer cooks or bakes.) As I went through the cards, I was reminded of some of my favorite childhood foods that she made—mushroom steak, cucumber and tomato salad, hush puppies, pralines—but it was the baked goods that registered the most vivid memories—chess pie, pecan pie, peach pie, lemon bars, oatmeal cake, chocolate cake. Many of the recipes were handwritten by her, and most had a date and source recorded to the side: "Molasses Pie from Sister, 1938"; "Sib's Date Bread, August 1954"; "20-Minute Fudge Cake from Dolly, 1962"; "Apple Sauce Cake, Mrs. Bradfield, Dec. 3, 1953"; "Chocolate Toll House

Cookies, May 20, 1971, made for Bible Study luncheon"; "Oatmeal Cake from Nannie, Christmas, 1961, made for bridge March 7, 1968." Some of the cards had notations such as "too much sugar," "bake at lower temperature," "This makes a very moist cake and is *very* [underlined twice] good!" After reading each one and recognizing some of the names that were inscribed, I felt I'd had an intimate glimpse into a part of my grandmother's life and of the people with whom she'd shared meals and swapped recipes.

While working on THE HARROWSMITH COUNTRY LIFE BAKING BOOK, I had a similar feeling, for this book turned out to be more than a collection of recipes; it, too, is like a family album—recorded through recipes rather than photographs and filled with memories of loved ones—mothers, fathers, sisters, sons, daughters, grandmothers, aunts, uncles, and friends. Both men and women responded to HARROWSMITH COUNTRY LIFE's request for favorite recipes for this baking book, and an overwhelming majority were accompanied by anecdotes about or acknowledgments to family members or friends, demonstrating that the love of baking is not only in the eating but also in the making, the giving, and the remembering.

To a great extent, this cookbook represents baking in the old style, with generous amounts of butter or margarine, brown sugar, sour cream, eggs, chocolate, nuts, and cream cheese; however, wholesome ingredients are in abundance as well, as are tips on adjusting some of the recipes so they fit these more health-conscious times. Ranging from pies, cakes, and cookies to muffins, rolls, and breads, there are baked goods for everyday needs, holidays, birthdays, spur-of-the-moment cravings, and gifts. Many can be made in large quantities and stored in the freezer, so there's always some delicious homemade treat on hand.

In order to select the very best recipes for this book, a staff of experienced cooks was hired to test more than 500 submissions, and then rate them as great, good, nothing special, or reject. Only those that received the highest marks are included. About half are for desserts; the others are for muffins, rolls, quick breads, and yeast breads that can be served for breakfast, lunch, or dinner.

Compiling this book required the help of a number of people. The family of friends and co-workers who assisted in its production include Camden House Publishing director Howard White, marketing coordinator Susan Walker, and administrative coordinator Nancy Sykes; designer Eugenie Delaney; illustrator Pamela Carroll; copy editor Faith Hanson; proofreaders Barb Jatkola and

Nan Fornal; typists Cathy Behrens, Margo Ketchum, and Linda Ottavi; type-setters Sheryl Fletcher and Chris Landry; photographer Becky Luigart-Stayner; food stylist Susan Herr; and the following recipe testers: Linda Bensinger, Corey Bensen, Sandra Cerda, Joyce Deveny, Priscilla Douglas, Beth Kellc, Diane Koss, Mark Makovec, Kim Martin, Tracy McGuinness, Mimi Powell, Deb Rossi, Peggy and Richard Roth, Sandra Roy, Jocelyn Secker-Walker, Gretchen Semuskie, Jean Spring, Jane Van Buren, Suzy White, and Debra Wright. Thank you all.

In addition, I want to thank my friend Richard Pisciotta, who helped me taste-test countless batches of cookies as well as muffins, quick breads, cakes, and pies. I also salute my mother, Dolly, sister, Sheryl, and stepmother, Dorothy, whose contributions extend well beyond the pages of this book.

Sandra J. Taylor
Hancock, New Hampshire
July 1992

PIES

HONEY APPLE PIE

ᏺ

Pastry for double-crust
  9-inch pie
6 cups unpeeled McIntosh
  apples, cored, thinly sliced
  lengthwise, then halved
½ cup sugar
¼ cup unbleached all-purpose
  flour
1 teaspoon cinnamon
1 tablespoon honey

This recipe was inspired by the baked apples that my grand-mother used to make in the fall. Whenever I bake this pie, I'm reminded not only of that wonderful taste and aroma but also of my childhood growing up in rural Georgia.

Place bottom crust in pie pan. Mix apples, sugar, flour, and cinnamon together, and pour into pie crust. Drizzle honey onto apples. Cover with top crust, seal, and make slits for venting. Place foil around edge of crust and bake pie in preheated 350°F oven for 45 to 55 minutes. (Remove foil for last 15 minutes of baking.)

Yield: One 9-inch pie.

Seleta Campbell
Chicago, Illinois

SUGARLESS APPLE PIE

ᏺ

2 tablespoons unbleached
  all-purpose flour
1 teaspoon cinnamon
¼ teaspoon salt
1 can (6 ounces) frozen apple
  juice concentrate, thawed
Pastry for double-crust 9-inch pie
5 to 6 firm baking apples
  (Jonathan, Cortland, etc.),
  peeled, cored, and sliced
2 tablespoons butter

Firm baking apples work best in this naturally sweetened pie. It makes an ideal dessert—luscious, easy to prepare, and pretty as a picture (see page 56).

In a saucepan, mix flour, cinnamon, and salt. Gradually add apple juice and heat until thickened. Place bottom crust in pie pan, add apple slices, and pour thickened apple juice over them. Dot with butter and cover with top crust, crimping edges together. Bake in preheated 450°F oven for 15 minutes. Reduce temperature to 350°F and bake 30 minutes longer, or until golden.

Yield: One 9-inch pie.

Norma Altaffer
Moorcroft, Wyoming

BLUEBERRY PIE

ટ&

FILLING
4 tablespoons unbleached
    all-purpose flour
1 teaspoon cinnamon
¼ teaspoon salt
1 cup sugar
2 cups blueberries
3 tablespoons butter, melted
1 teaspoon vanilla

CRUST
2 cups unbleached
    all-purpose flour
1 teaspoon salt
⅔ cup shortening
8 tablespoons ice water
    (approximately)

This pie is fantastic with blueberries, but if you can't find them, don't hesitate to substitute another kind of berry, such as blackberries, boysenberries, or dewberries. When making the crust, be sure the water you use is ice cold. Add a few cubes of ice to the water and stir until well chilled.

For the filling, mix together flour, cinnamon, salt, and sugar. Add blueberries and toss lightly. Stir in melted butter and vanilla, mixing until berries are well coated. Set aside for 15 minutes, or until crust is ready to fill.

In large bowl, sift together flour and salt. Cut in shortening with pastry blender until mixture resembles cornmeal. Add the ice water, a tablespoon at a time, stirring with a fork until dough is manageable.

Divide dough in half and roll out on floured surface. Place bottom crust in 9-inch pie pan, cutting edge of dough evenly with outside edge of pan. Pour in filling, cover with lattice crust, and seal edges, making a high, fluted rim.

Bake in preheated 450°F oven for 15 minutes, then reduce temperature to 375°F and bake 25 to 30 minutes more. (If crust browns too quickly, reduce temperature to 350°F.)

Yield: One 9-inch pie.

Dorothy Taylor
Houston, Texas

CRUNCHY-TOP PEACH PIE

ஓ

FILLING

2 tablespoons unbleached
  all-purpose flour
½ teaspoon cinnamon
Dash or two of nutmeg
4 cups peeled, pitted, and sliced
  peaches (well drained if canned)
Juice of 1 lemon
½ cup honey
Pastry for single-crust
  9-inch pie
1 egg yolk, beaten

TOPPING

2 cups rolled oats
½ teaspoon cinnamon
½ cup chopped almonds
¼ cup unbleached
  all-purpose flour
Pinch of salt
5 tablespoons unsalted butter
3 tablespoons honey

This can be made any time of the year, but it's at its best when ripe, juicy, fresh peaches are used. Serve warm with a scoop of vanilla ice cream.

To prepare the filling, mix flour, cinnamon, and nutmeg, and toss with peaches until evenly coated. Drizzle with lemon juice and honey, and mix well. Place pastry in pie pan, brush with egg yolk, and pour in peach mixture.

For the topping, combine oats, cinnamon, almonds, flour, and salt. In a small pan, melt butter and honey, then stir into oats mixture, blending well. Pour over peach filling and pat firmly into place. Bake in preheated 400°F oven for 25 to 30 minutes, covering crust with foil if it begins to brown too quickly.

Yield: One 9-inch pie.

*Mattie Taylor
Stout, Ohio*

HONEY PEACH PIE

Pastry for double-crust
   9-inch pie
3 cups ripe peaches, peeled,
   pitted, and sliced
¼ cup honey
1 tablespoon unbleached
   all-purpose flour
¼ teaspoon salt
½ teaspoon cinnamon
¼ teaspoon nutmeg
2 tablespoons butter or margarine

This is so easy to prepare it doesn't have to be reserved for special occasions.

Line pie pan with bottom crust, fill with peaches, and drizzle with honey. Combine flour, salt, cinnamon, and nutmeg, and sprinkle over top. Dot with butter and cover with top crust.

Using a fork, perforate crust several times. Bake in preheated 450°F oven for 10 minutes, reduce temperature to 375°F, and continue baking for 20 to 25 minutes, or until crust is done.

Yield: One 9-inch pie.

Cassandra Reeves
Auburn, California

PEAR PIE

3 to 4 medium pears
Juice of ½ lemon
Pastry for single-crust
   9-inch pie
Angostura bitters (optional)
¼ cup (½ stick) butter or
   margarine, softened
1 cup sugar
¼ cup unbleached
   all-purpose flour
3 eggs
1 teaspoon vanilla
⅛ teaspoon salt (optional)
⅛ teaspoon nutmeg or mace

A creamy, custardlike filling surrounds the pears, which are firm and full of flavor. (See page 53.)

Peel, halve, and core pears. Brush with lemon juice. Place pear halves cut side down in pastry-lined pie pan with narrow ends toward the center. Put a dash of bitters on each half, if desired.

Cream together butter and sugar. Beat in flour, eggs, vanilla, and salt, if using. Pour mixture over pears and sprinkle lightly with nutmeg or mace. Bake in preheated 350°F oven for 45 minutes, or until filling is set and lightly browned. Cool for at least 1 hour before cutting.

Yield: One 9-inch pie.

Mark E. Williams
Salisbury, Maryland

STAINED-GLASS PIE

ɚ

1 cup pitted and quartered prunes
1 cup dried apricots
½ cup golden raisins
1 cup halved cranberries
1 cup peeled, cored, and
   chopped tart apples
½ cup coarsely chopped walnuts
¼ cup (½ stick) margarine
⅓ cup sugar
¼ cup orange juice
Pastry for double-crust
   9-inch pie
¼ cup orange marmalade
1 teaspoon orange juice

A beautiful dessert for Thanksgiving or Christmas dinner. The colors will shine through if you top it with a lattice crust.

In a 3-quart heavy saucepan, combine prunes, apricots, and raisins. Add enough water to cover fruit. Bring to a boil, reduce heat to simmer, and cook uncovered for 10 minutes, or until tender. Drain. Add cranberries, apples, nuts, margarine, sugar, and ¼ cup orange juice. Cook, stirring constantly, for 5 minutes. Cover and refrigerate at least 2 hours or overnight to mellow flavors.

Place bottom crust in pie pan and spoon in filling. In a small saucepan, heat marmalade and 1 teaspoon orange juice. Strain and drizzle over filling.

For lattice top, roll out top crust and cut into 10 strips. Place on filling in lattice pattern, trimming ends evenly with bottom crust. Press edges together and flute.

Bake in preheated 400°F oven for 45 to 55 minutes, or until filling in center is bubbly. (Cover pie edge with foil, if necessary, to prevent overbrowning.)

Yield: One 9-inch pie.

Darlene Markel
Roseburg, Oregon

COMPANY PIE

❧

Pastry for double-crust
  9-inch pie
1 cup mincemeat
2 cups whole cranberries
2 cups peeled, cored, and sliced
  tart apples
⅔ cup sugar (or to taste)
1½ teaspoons Chinese Five
  Spice seasoning
3 tablespoons unbleached
  all-purpose flour
Milk
Sugar

This simple recipe combines a trio of holiday flavors into a delectable dessert for a special meal (see page 53).

Line a deep pie pan with bottom crust and spoon in mincemeat, spreading evenly. Toss together cranberries, apples, sugar, spice, and flour, and distribute over mincemeat. Cover with top crust, flute edges, and cut steam vents. Brush top crust with a little milk and sprinkle with sugar. Bake in preheated 375°F oven for 35 to 40 minutes, or until filling bubbles through vents. Serve warm or cold with thin slices of cheese.

Yield: 1 deep-dish 9-inch pie.

Irene Wood
Fairbanks, Alaska

RAISIN PIE

❧

2 cups raisins
2 cups water
2 tablespoons cornstarch
½ cup sugar
2 teaspoons grated lemon zest
3 tablespoons lemon juice
Pastry for single-crust
  9-inch pie
Butter

Unlike most recipes for raisin pie, which have a creamy filling, this one consists mostly of raisins. Lemon zest and lemon juice complement the sweetness.

Heat raisins and water to boiling. Mix together cornstarch and sugar, and stir into raisin mixture. Cook over medium heat, stirring constantly, until mixture thickens and boils. Remove from heat and stir in lemon zest and juice. Pour into pastry-lined pie pan and dot with butter. Bake in preheated 375°F oven for about 45 minutes.

Yield: One 9-inch pie.

Sharon Evans
Rockwell, Iowa

SWEET-POTATO PIE

෫

2½ cups baked, mashed
   sweet potatoes
3 tablespoons butter, softened
½ cup granulated sugar
1 cup packed brown sugar
4 eggs
1 teaspoon nutmeg
½ teaspoon cinnamon
½ teaspoon salt
½ teaspoon lemon extract
1 cup half-and-half
Pastry for 2 single-crust
   9-inch pies

At holidays, reunions, and socials throughout the South, you'll always find sweet-potato pies among the desserts. This is one of the best.

In a large bowl, beat together sweet potatoes, butter, sugars, eggs, spices, salt, lemon extract, and half-and-half. (Mixture may be a little thin.) Divide the filling equally between 2 pastry-lined pans and bake in preheated 450°F oven for 10 minutes. Reduce temperature to 350°F and bake for 45 minutes, or until toothpick inserted near center comes out clean.

Yield: Two 9-inch pies.

Stan Shawhart
Arthur City, Texas

OATMEAL PIE

෫

3 eggs, beaten
⅔ cup granulated sugar
1 cup packed brown sugar
⅔ cup quick-cooking oats
⅔ cup shredded coconut
⅓ cup milk
2 tablespoons margarine
   or butter, melted
1 teaspoon vanilla
1 teaspoon cinnamon
Pastry for single-crust
   9-inch pie

I'm always asked to make this for Thanksgiving and Christmas. It's very rich and has the texture of pecan pie.

Stir together eggs, sugars, oats, coconut, milk, margarine, vanilla, and cinnamon, mixing until well blended. Pour filling into pastry-lined pie pan and bake in preheated 350°F oven for 35 minutes. Be careful not to overbake.

Yield: One 9-inch pie.

Lynn Clubb
What Cheer, Iowa

PUMPKIN-ORANGE PIE IN A WALNUT CRUST

🐌

CRUST
1 cup whole-wheat flour
1 cup ground walnuts
3 tablespoons oil
¼ cup orange juice or water
½ teaspoon cinnamon

FILLING
2 cups cooked, mashed pumpkin
1½ cups plain yogurt
½ cup orange juice
¼ cup brown sugar
½ cup granulated sugar
2 eggs, beaten
½ teaspoon salt
1 teaspoon cinnamon
½ teaspoon ginger
¼ teaspoon nutmeg
¼ teaspoon allspice
⅛ teaspoon cloves
1 tablespoon grated orange zest

A flavorful combination of pumpkin and citrus in a nutty crust. Using low-fat or nonfat yogurt instead of the usual evaporated milk or cream makes this a healthier dessert.

Combine crust ingredients and press into a 9-inch pie pan. Set aside.

To make the filling, beat together pumpkin, yogurt, orange juice, sugars, and eggs. Add salt, spices, and orange zest, and stir until thoroughly blended. Pour into pastry-lined pie pan. Bake in preheated 425°F oven for 15 minutes, lower temperature to 350°F, and continue baking for 45 minutes, or until knife inserted in the middle comes out clean.

Yield: One 9-inch pie.

Amy Shortlidge   *Mark Newman*
East Falmouth, Massachusetts   *and*   *Ithaca, New York*

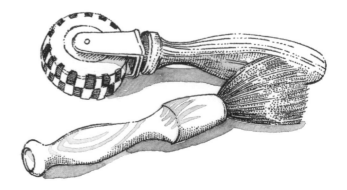

MILLMOSS PIE (CARAMEL-TOPPED SQUASH PIE)

ક્ર

1 cup plain cottage cheese
1 can (15 ounces) squash (or 2
    cups cooked and pureed fresh
    squash)
¼ cup milk
2 eggs
½ cup sugar
1 tablespoon unbleached
    all-purpose flour
½ teaspoon ginger (or to taste)
½ teaspoon cinnamon (or to taste)
½ teaspoon cloves (or to taste)
Pastry for single-crust
    9-inch pie

CARAMEL TOPPING
1 tablespoon margarine
½ cup brown sugar
1 cup whole pecans

This pie is incredibly simple to prepare and makes a beautiful presentation. Any kind of plain cottage cheese can be used—low-fat, large-curd, small-curd, or creamed—just be sure it's plain and not a variety that contains pineapple or other ingredients.

Place cottage cheese in a blender or food processor and mix until smooth. Add the squash, milk, eggs, sugar, flour, and spices, and blend until well mixed. Pour filling into pastry-lined pie pan and bake in preheated 350°F oven for 35 to 40 minutes, or until set.

Remove pie from oven and prepare the topping. In small skillet or pan, heat together margarine and brown sugar until melted and thoroughly blended. Add pecans and stir until well coated. Drizzle around top edge of baked pie filling, distributing pecans evenly.

Yield: One 9-inch pie.

*B. A. Millmoss
Hancock, New Hampshire*

FRESH COCONUT PIE

≥.

3 eggs
1½ cups sugar
½ cup (1 stick) butter or
    margarine, melted
1 tablespoon lemon juice
1 teaspoon vanilla
1 fresh whole coconut, meat
    removed and shredded
    (or 7-ounce bag)
Pastry for single-crust
    9-inch pie

This pie is special because it is my husband's favorite. It's not a cream pie, but it's sinfully rich nonetheless. Use fresh coconut if you can find it.

Beat eggs and sugar until fluffy. Add cooled melted butter, lemon juice, and vanilla, and continue beating until well blended. Stir in coconut. Pour into pastry-lined pie pan and bake in preheated 350°F oven for about 1 hour.

Yield: One 9-inch pie.

Marcia Ann Thornton
Los Lunas, New Mexico

RHUBARB CREAM PIE

≥.

FILLING
4 egg yolks, beaten
4 tablespoons cornstarch
¼ teaspoon salt
2½ cups sugar
½ cup light cream
    (or evaporated milk)
4 tablespoons butter, melted
4 cups diced rhubarb
Pastry for deep-dish, single-crust
    10-inch pie

MERINGUE TOPPING
4 egg whites
1¼ teaspoons cream of tartar
8 tablespoons sugar

My mother has made this pie for as long as I can remember. Now that I have little girls myself, I enjoy making it for them.

In large pot, mix egg yolks, cornstarch, salt, sugar, and cream. Stir in cooled melted butter and rhubarb, and cook until thickened and rhubarb is tender, about 10 to 15 minutes. Cool mixture, then pour into pastry-lined pie pan.

To make topping, beat egg whites until foamy. Add cream of tartar and beat until soft peaks form. Gradually add sugar, beating until stiff and glossy. Spread over filling and bake in preheated 275°F oven for 25 to 30 minutes, or until lightly browned on top.

Yield: One 10-inch pie.

Pat Nelson
Cody, Wyoming

SPICED RHUBARB-STRAWBERRY PIE

৵

3 cups cut-up rhubarb
   (¾-inch pieces)
1 pint strawberries,
   cut in half
¾ cup sugar
2 tablespoons cornstarch
⅛ teaspoon salt
¼ teaspoon pumpkin-pie spice
   or mace
Pastry for double-crust
   9-inch pie
2 tablespoons margarine

This is a great way to use a huge crop of rhubarb in the spring. I mix up several batches of the filling and freeze them for pies all summer long.

Combine rhubarb and strawberries in bowl. Sprinkle on sugar, cornstarch, salt, and spice; mix gently. Turn into pastry-lined pie pan and dot with margarine. Make lattice top with remaining crust, flute edges, and bake in preheated 400°F oven for 40 to 45 minutes. Cool on rack before serving.

Yield: One 9-inch pie.

Lynette Herlan
Fall City, Washington

CHERRY-BERRY PIE

৵

1⅓ cups pitted cherries
1⅓ cups blueberries
1⅓ cups raspberries or strawberries
   (the latter cut in half)
1 cup sugar (more or less,
   depending on sweetness
   of berries)
⅓ cup unbleached
   all-purpose flour
½ teaspoon cinnamon
Pastry for double-crust
   9-inch pie
2 tablespoons butter

Just about any berry combination will work in this, so use whatever is in season and select the spice that best complements the fruits.

In large bowl, combine cherries and berries. Add sugar, flour, and cinnamon, and toss to coat fruit. Pour into pastry-lined pie pan, dot with butter, and cover with lattice top. Bake in preheated 450°F oven for 10 minutes, then reduce temperature to 350°F, and bake 30 minutes more, or until crust is golden.

Yield: One 9-inch pie.

Sy Montgomery
Hancock, New Hampshire

LEMON PIE

ᴁ

CRUST
1½ cups unbleached
   all-purpose flour
½ teaspoon salt (or less to taste)
½ cup shortening
4 to 5 tablespoons cold water

FILLING
1½ cups sugar
3 tablespoons cornstarch
3 tablespoons unbleached
   all-purpose flour
Dash of salt
1½ cups hot water
3 egg yolks, beaten
2 tablespoons butter
½ teaspoon grated lemon zest
⅓ cup lemon juice

MERINGUE
3 egg whites
1 teaspoon lemon juice
6 tablespoons sugar

Growing up in southern California, we always had a Meyer lemon tree in our yard. This recipe was perfected by my mother. Four generations have loved it—a taste of sunny California.

To make the crust, combine flour and salt with the shortening until mixture is crumbly. Gradually add the cold water until dough forms a ball. Roll out on well-floured board and place in 10-inch pie pan. Prick bottom and sides with a fork and bake at 450°F for 10 to 12 minutes.

To make the filling, combine sugar, cornstarch, flour, and salt in medium-size saucepan, gradually stir in hot water, and quickly bring to boil, stirring constantly. Reduce heat and cook 8 minutes. Stir small amount of hot mixture into the beaten egg yolks, then pour back into saucepan. Boil 4 minutes, stirring constantly. Add butter, lemon zest, and lemon juice, and stir to blend. Pour into cooled, baked pastry shell and bring to room temperature.

To make meringue, beat egg whites with lemon juice to form soft peaks. Gradually add sugar, beating until stiff peaks form and sugar has dissolved. Spread meringue over filling, spreading to edges. Bake in preheated 350°F oven for 12 to 15 minutes. Cool before serving.

Yield: One 10-inch pie.

Peggy Flocken
Layton, Utah

CHOCOLATE PIE

ò

FILLING
2 cups sugar
6 tablespoons cocoa
¾ cup unbleached
 all-purpose flour
4 cups milk
8 egg yolks
3 teaspoons vanilla
6 tablespoons butter
Pastry for single-crust
 10-inch pie, baked

MERINGUE TOPPING
2 tablespoons cornstarch
4 tablespoons sugar
½ cup water
8 egg whites
Dash of salt
¾ cup plus 2 tablespoons sugar

This pie is rich and creamy . . . a dream come true for chocolate lovers, and I'm one of those.

To prepare the filling, combine sugar, cocoa, and flour in the top of a double boiler. Add 1 cup of the milk and mix.

In a bowl, beat egg yolks with 2 cups of the milk. Add to cocoa-flour mixture along with the last cup of milk. Cook over boiling water until mixture thickens, about 25 to 30 minutes, stirring from time to time. Remove from heat, add vanilla and butter, and stir until blended. Set aside while making topping.

To prepare the topping, mix cornstarch, sugar, and water in saucepan, and cook over low heat until thick and clear. Set aside to cool. Beat egg whites and salt until soft peaks form. Add sugar, 1 tablespoon at a time, beating until whites are stiff. Add cooled cornstarch mixture.

Pour filling into baked crust, cover with meringue, and bake in preheated 350°F oven for 20 to 30 minutes.

Yield: One 10-inch pie.

Susan S. Lee
Louisville, Kentucky

PECAN FUDGE PIE

જ

½ cup (1 stick) butter or
   margarine
3 squares (1 ounce each)
   unsweetened chocolate
4 eggs
2 tablespoons unbleached
   all-purpose flour
3 tablespoons corn syrup
2 cups sugar
¼ teaspoon salt
1 teaspoon vanilla
1 cup chopped pecans
Pastry for single-crust
   9-inch pie

Although this pie is absolutely heavenly just as it is, we also love it topped with whipped cream or vanilla ice cream.

Melt butter and chocolate in double boiler or heavy-bottomed pot, stirring to blend. Remove from heat and set aside to cool.

In large bowl, beat eggs lightly. Add flour, corn syrup, sugar, salt, and vanilla, and mix well. Gradually stir in cooled chocolate mixture, beating until thoroughly combined. Fold in pecans. Pour filling into pastry-lined pie pan and bake in preheated 350°F oven for 30 to 35 minutes. Do not overbake.

Yield: One 9-inch pie.

*Burnette Boyett
Houston, Texas*

SHERRY'S PECAN PIE

જ

1¼ cups brown sugar
½ cup corn syrup
¼ cup (½ stick) butter
3 eggs
1 cup pecans
Pastry for single-crust
   9-inch pie

This pie is rich not only in color and taste, but also in memories — of my grandparents, who had pecan trees in their yard. After carefully cracking and shelling bags full of these nuts, they shared the harvest with family members and friends.

Combine sugar, corn syrup, and butter in heavy-bottomed pot and bring to a boil, stirring constantly. Remove from heat and set aside to cool.

In medium-size bowl, beat eggs thoroughly. Slowly add cooled syrup mixture, beating continuously. Stir in pecans and pour into pastry-lined pie pan. Bake in preheated 350°F oven for 40 to 45 minutes.

Yield: One 9-inch pie.

*Sherry Hochmann
San Antonio, Texas*

PECAN TARTS

⅛

½ cup (1 stick) butter, softened
1 package (3 ounces) cream
   cheese, softened
1 cup unbleached
   all-purpose flour
1 egg
½ teaspoon vanilla
¾ cup packed dark brown sugar
1 tablespoon margarine, melted
1 cup chopped pecans

This recipe came to me from the mother of a young man I briefly dated. Although our romance didn't last, this recipe certainly has.

Mix together butter, cream cheese, and flour. Divide and shape into 24 balls, flatten with heel of hand, and press into the ungreased cups of tart pans.

Beat egg, vanilla, brown sugar, and margarine until well blended. Stir in pecans. Fill tart shells with filling and bake in preheated 350°F oven for 15 to 20 minutes, or until crust is lightly browned.

Yield: 24 tarts.

Mary Jane Helgerson
FPO-AE

PIE CRUST

⅛

3 cups unbleached
   all-purpose flour
1 teaspoon salt
1¼ cups shortening, divided
1 egg
2 teaspoons vinegar
5 tablespoons water

This is the most-requested recipe I have. It is very easy to make, and the dough freezes well.

Combine flour and salt in a large bowl, add ½ cup of the shortening, and cut finely with pastry blender. Cut in remaining shortening.

Beat egg, mix with vinegar and water, and add to flour mixture, blending well. Shape into 3 or 4 balls, and gently roll out dough on floured surface or wax paper. Line 3 or 4 pie pans with pastry and freeze until ready to use.

To bake crust without a filling, prick pastry all over with fork, and bake in preheated 450°F oven for 10 to 12 minutes.

Yield: Four 8-inch or three 9-inch crusts.

Lea A. Scheid
Glen Ellyn, Illinois

NO-FAIL PIE CRUST

❧

2½ cups unbleached
    all-purpose flour
1 tablespoon sugar
1 teaspoon salt
1 cup shortening
1 egg yolk, beaten
Milk

In addition to dessert pies, this crust can be used with savory pies and quiches. Add a tablespoon of celery seeds, poppy seeds, or sesame seeds, depending on the filling.

Sift together flour, sugar, and salt. Cut in shortening. Put egg yolk in a measuring cup and add enough milk to measure ⅔ cup. Add to flour mixture and blend. If dough is sticky, add a bit of flour for ease of handling. Shape into 4 balls and roll out on a lightly floured surface.

Yield: Four 9-inch crusts.

Nancy Ritchey
Newport News, Virginia

NO-FAIL FLAKY PIE CRUST

❧

3 cups unbleached
    all-purpose flour
1 teaspoon salt
¼ teaspoon baking powder
1¼ cups shortening
1 egg
4 to 6 tablespoons cold water
1 tablespoon white vinegar

Before I tried this recipe, I couldn't make a decent pie crust. Now it's a delight, and every one is a success. Honest!

Combine dry ingredients and cut in shortening. In a separate bowl, beat together egg, 4 tablespoons water, and vinegar. Add to flour mixture and blend together well. Add 1 to 2 tablespoons more water if needed. (Depending on the weather, you may need to chill the dough for a while before rolling it out.)

Divide dough into quarters and roll out each on floured surface or between wax paper to desired size.

Yield: Four 9-inch crusts.

Mary Novotny
Eugene, Oregon

QUANTITY PIE CRUST

&.

4 cups unbleached
   all-purpose flour
1¾ cups shortening
1 tablespoon sugar
2 teaspoons salt
1 tablespoon white vinegar
1 egg
½ cup water

It is no more trouble to make dough for five pie crusts than it is for one. This freezes unbaked in very little space and cannot be damaged, as a baked crust can. The crust browns well and is light and flaky.

In a large bowl and using a fork or pastry blender, cut together flour, shortening, sugar, and salt. In separate bowl, beat together vinegar, egg, and water, and add to flour mixture. Stir with fork until all ingredients are moistened. Shape dough into a ball and chill at least 15 minutes before rolling.

After chilling, divide dough into 5 portions for 9-inch pies or 4 portions for 10-inch pies. Roll out a portion at a time between sheets of wax paper. Refrigerate for up to 3 days, or freeze until needed, each portion wrapped individually.

Yield: Five 9-inch or four 10-inch crusts.

Ellen H. Gailey
Albuquerque, New Mexico

CAKES

Black Forest Cheesecake

❧

1½ cups crushed chocolate
   wafers (or 18 Oreo cookies)
¼ cup (½ stick) butter or
   margarine, melted
3 packages (8 ounces each)
   cream cheese, softened
1½ cups sugar
4 eggs
⅓ cup cherry-flavored liqueur
4 squares (1 ounce each)
   semi-sweet chocolate
½ cup sour cream
   (or nonfat yogurt)
1 can (21 ounces) cherry pie
   filling
Whipped cream
Maraschino cherries with stems
¼ cup chopped walnuts

This dessert is beautiful and delicious (see page 132). It can be made the night before, then refrigerated until right before serving, when the finishing touches are added.

Combine crushed wafers and melted butter, and press firmly into bottom of 9-inch springform pan. Beat cream cheese until light, then gradually add sugar. Add eggs, one at a time, blending well. Stir in liqueur and pour into prepared pan. Bake in preheated 350°F oven for 1 hour. Remove from oven and let cake cool to room temperature.

Place chocolate in top of double boiler. Bring water to a boil, reduce temperature to low, and heat until chocolate melts. Cool slightly and stir in sour cream. Spread chocolate mixture over top of cooled cheesecake.

Just before serving, spread pie filling over chocolate layer, put large spoonfuls of whipped cream evenly around top edge of cheesecake, and place a cherry in each mound of cream. Sprinkle chopped walnuts around edge and over whipped cream and cherries.

Yield: 16 to 18 servings.

Janice Hewett
Murray, Nebraska

CRUSTLESS CHOCOLATE CHEESECAKE

ᔏ

3 packages (8 ounces each) cream cheese, softened
1 can (14 ounces) sweetened condensed milk
12-ounce package semi-sweet chocolate chips, melted
4 eggs
2 teaspoons vanilla (or crème de menthe or crème de cacao)

Quick and easy, rich and creamy, this luscious cheesecake can stand on its own — without crust or topping. If, however, you want to dress it up, add a little vanilla or liqueur to heavy cream, beat to desired consistency, and adorn each serving with a small dollop.

Butter a 9-inch springform pan and wrap the outside with double layers of aluminum foil to seal the bottom. Preheat oven to 325°F.

In large bowl, beat cream cheese until fluffy. Gradually add condensed milk, mixing until smooth. Stir in melted chocolate and then add eggs, one at a time, blending well. Mix in vanilla.

Pour into prepared springform pan and set inside a larger pan. Add enough hot water to outer pan so it comes halfway up sides of springform pan. Bake in hot-water bath for about 50 to 60 minutes, or until center is just set.

Remove springform pan to rack and cool completely. Run knife around inside edge of pan, then open hinge to release sides. Chill for a few hours before serving.

Yield: 12 to 16 servings.

Anne Pisciotta
Huntington, New York

COMPANY CHEESECAKE

&.

CRUST
1¾ cups graham-cracker crumbs
¼ to ⅓ cup ground hazelnuts
½ teaspoon cinnamon
½ cup (1 stick) butter, melted
2 teaspoons sugar
Dash of nutmeg
Dash of cloves
Dash of cardamom

FILLING
3 eggs, well beaten
2 packages (8 ounces each)
  cream cheese, softened
1 cup sugar
¼ teaspoon salt
2 teaspoons vanilla
½ teaspoon almond extract
⅛ teaspoon cardamom
3 cups sour cream

The combination of hazelnuts, cardamom, and almond extract creates an unusual and delightful flavor. See if your guests can guess what the ingredients are.

Combine crust ingredients and mix thoroughly. Press onto bottom and sides (up about 2½ inches) of a 9-inch springform pan, and set aside.

Combine all filling ingredients except sour cream and beat until smooth. (A food processor works great.) Blend in sour cream and pour into crust. Using a knife, trim crust above filling and let crumbs fall around edge to decorate. Bake in preheated 375°F oven for 45 to 60 minutes, or until just set. Sides may puff slightly. Let cool to room temperature, then chill well for 4 to 5 hours before serving. The filling will be softer than most other cheesecakes.

Yield: 12 to 14 servings.

Katharyn Risley Hoke
Elkins, New Hampshire

CHIFFON CAKE

2 cups sifted unbleached
  all-purpose flour
1½ cups sugar
3 teaspoons baking powder
1 teaspoon salt
½ cup oil
5 egg yolks
¾ cup cold water
2 teaspoons vanilla
2 teaspoons grated lemon zest
1 cup egg whites (7 to 8)
½ teaspoon cream of tartar

LEMON GLAZE (optional)
1½ cups confectioners' sugar
4½ tablespoons lemon juice

An elegant and professional-looking cake (see cover). If desired, drizzle the top and sides with tangy Lemon Glaze.

Sift together flour, sugar, baking powder, and salt. Make a well in dry ingredients and add oil, egg yolks, water, vanilla, and lemon zest. Beat until smooth. In large mixing bowl, whip egg whites and cream of tartar until very stiff peaks form. Gradually pour egg-yolk mixture over whipped whites, gently folding with rubber spatula just until blended. Pour into ungreased 10-inch tube pan.

Bake in preheated 325°F oven for 55 minutes, then increase to 350°F, and bake for 10 to 15 minutes more. Invert until cool. Remove to cake plate and, if desired, drizzle with glaze, made by whisking together until smooth confectioners' sugar and lemon juice.

Yield: 16 to 20 servings.

Pauline Manowski
Stevens Point, Wisconsin

BLACKBERRY JAM CAKE

1 cup granulated sugar
1 cup brown sugar
1 cup shortening
6 eggs
1 cup buttermilk
2 teaspoons baking soda
3 cups unbleached all-purpose
  flour, sifted
3 cups blackberry jam
2 teaspoons cinnamon
2 teaspoons nutmeg
(continued)

A moist cake that keeps well if stored in an airtight container. The icing is creamy — almost like candy — and is equally delicious on apple or spice cake.

Line two 8-inch cake pans with wax paper, then grease and flour them. Preheat oven to 325°F.

In large bowl, cream sugars and shortening. Add eggs, two at a time, and beat well. In small bowl, combine buttermilk and baking soda. Add to the creamed mixture alternately with the flour, then stir in jam and spices. Pour into prepared pans and bake for 40 to 60 minutes.

To make icing, combine brown sugar, half-and-half, and cream of tartar in heavy-bottomed pot, and cook to soft-

CARAMEL ICING
2 cups brown sugar
¾ cup half-and-half
Pinch of cream of tartar
1 tablespoon butter
¼ teaspoon vanilla

ball stage. Remove from heat and stir in butter and vanilla. Let cool to lukewarm, then beat hard until mixture is creamy. (This requires some "elbow power" but is worth the effort.) If mixture becomes too thick, stir in a small amount of half-and-half. Spread over cooled cake.

Yield: 8 to 10 servings.

Ruby B. Vice
Carlisle, Kentucky

ORANGE CAKE

ᐠᐟ

½ cup orange juice
½ cup milk
2 cups unbleached
  all-purpose flour
1½ cups sugar
½ teaspoon baking soda
1 teaspoon salt
3 teaspoons baking powder
½ cup shortening
1 tablespoon grated orange zest
2 eggs

One of our recipe testers brought this cake into the office at HARROWSMITH COUNTRY LIFE, where a number of staff members sampled it themselves. It received consistently high marks for taste, texture, and the right amount of sweetness.

In measuring cup, combine orange juice and milk. Into large bowl, sift together flour, sugar, soda, salt, and baking powder. Add shortening, orange zest, and all but ⅓ cup of the combined juice and milk. Beat 2 minutes. Add eggs and remaining juice/milk combination, and beat 2 minutes more.

Pour into greased and floured 10-inch tube pan. Bake in preheated 350°F oven for 25 to 30 minutes, or until a toothpick inserted in center comes out clean. Cool, then remove from pan. Sprinkle with confectioners' sugar, or frost as desired.

Yield: 12 servings.

Donna Mutchler
Bethlehem, Pennsylvania

PEACHES & CHEESE CAKE

&

CAKE

1 cup unbleached
   all-purpose flour
½ cup sugar
½ teaspoon baking powder
½ cup (1 stick) butter or
   margarine, cut into
   ½-inch slices
2 eggs
1 teaspoon grated lemon zest

FILLING

1 can (29 to 32 ounces) sliced
   peaches, drained
1 package (8 ounces)
   cream cheese, cut in eighths
½ cup sugar
2 eggs
2 teaspoons lemon juice
½ cup sour cream

TOPPING

½ cup raspberry jam

This was developed for a family member who didn't like graham-cracker crusts. It's not quite so "cheesy" as are traditional cheesecakes and has a good balance of fruit. When I canned a lot, home-canned peaches and freezer-fresh jam made this a real treat at our house.

Using full-size food processor, with S-blade in bowl, make the cake layer by processing flour, sugar, and baking powder for 2 to 3 pulses, to mix. With processor running, drop cold butter slices through feed tube, one at a time, and process until the mixture is crumbly. Add eggs and lemon zest, and process until smooth. Spread evenly into greased 9x13-inch pan.

For the filling, arrange well-drained sliced peaches (about 3 cups) evenly on top of batter. In same processor bowl, mix cream cheese, sugar, eggs, and lemon juice for 1 minute. Scrape down sides of bowl with rubber spatula and process until mixture is smooth and creamy. Stir in sour cream (do not beat) and spoon over peaches.

Bake in preheated 350°F oven for 15 minutes. Reduce temperature to 300°F and remove from oven. Spoon jam, ½ teaspoon at a time, over the top. Return to oven and bake another 20 to 25 minutes. Cool thoroughly on rack and refrigerate for at least 2 hours before serving.

Yield: 18 servings.

Adeline Halfmann
Campbellsport, Wisconsin

SPECIAL-TREAT CHEESECAKE

❧

CRUST

¾ cup finely chopped
   unsalted cashews
¾ cup finely chopped pecans
¾ cup rolled oats
¾ cup whole-wheat flour
¾ cup date sugar (or turbinado)
½ cup (1 stick) butter, melted
¼ cup maple syrup
1 teaspoon vanilla
Dash of almond extract

FILLING

4 packages (8 ounces each)
   cream cheese, softened
½ cup honey
½ cup maple syrup
1½ tablespoons lemon juice
½ tablespoon vanilla
¾ cup half-and-half
3 tablespoons well-beaten egg

This cheesecake is somewhat expensive and very rich—thus the name of the recipe. It has become a tradition in our family to make this once a year for the Christmas and New Year holidays, which makes it even more special.

To make crust, mix cashews, pecans, oats, whole-wheat flour, and date sugar in large bowl. In separate bowl, combine butter, maple syrup, vanilla, and almond extract. Add to flour and nuts, and stir until well blended. Spoon mixture into 9-inch springform pan and press firmly onto bottom and partway up sides. Bake in preheated 350°F oven for 10 minutes. Remove from oven and set aside.

For the filling, beat softened cream cheese until smooth. Combine honey, maple syrup, lemon juice, and vanilla, then mix into cream cheese. Beat together half-and-half and egg, and fold into cream cheese mixture. Spoon onto crust and spread evenly, smoothing the top. Bake at 350°F for 60 to 75 minutes, or until just set. Let cool completely, then refrigerate until thoroughly chilled.

Yield: 16 to 18 servings.

Milan Radan
Port Townsend, Washington

GREEK WALNUT CAKES

ò.

1½ cups sifted unbleached
   all-purpose flour
2 teaspoons baking powder
1 teaspoon cinnamon
¼ teaspoon salt
1 cup (2 sticks) butter
   or margarine, softened
1 cup sugar
4 eggs
1 tablespoon grated orange zest
⅓ cup orange juice
2 cups finely chopped walnuts
24 walnut halves

HONEY SYRUP
2-inch piece orange zest
½ cup sugar
½ cup water
1-inch cinnamon stick
½ cup honey

These rich and moist cakes look pretty set out on a party table. They store well and make wonderful gifts, too.

Sift flour, baking powder, cinnamon, and salt together. In separate bowl, beat butter with sugar until well blended. Beat in eggs, one at a time, until mixture is light and fluffy. Stir in orange zest. Add flour mixture alternately with orange juice, beating after each addition until batter is smooth. Stir in chopped walnuts.

Pour into buttered 9x13-inch pan and bake in preheated 350°F oven for about 30 minutes. While cake bakes, prepare the syrup. Combine orange zest (no white), sugar, water, and cinnamon stick. Bring to a boil, lower heat, and simmer 25 minutes. Stir in honey and blend well. Remove orange zest and cinnamon stick, and cool.

When cake is done, remove to wire rack and cool for 10 minutes. Gradually pour cool syrup over cake, letting syrup soak in before adding more.

To serve, cut cake into twenty-four 2-inch squares, put each square in fluted foil baking cup, and top each with walnut half.

Yield: 2 dozen squares.

Kathy Springer
Trumansburg, New York

ORANGE CARROT CAKE

ಜಿ

3 cups flour
2 cups sugar
1 cup shredded coconut
2½ teaspoons baking soda
2½ teaspoons cinnamon
1 teaspoon salt
2 cups shredded carrots
  (4 medium)
1½ cups oil
2 teaspoons vanilla
3 eggs
1 teaspoon grated orange zest
1 can (11 ounces) mandarin
  oranges, drained

CREAM CHEESE FROSTING
1 package (8 ounces)
  cream cheese, softened
2 tablespoons butter or
  margarine, softened
1 teaspoon vanilla
3 cups confectioners' sugar
½ to 1 cup chopped nuts

A moist, sweet variation on a familiar theme. To bring out the orange flavor even more, try a bit of grated orange zest in the frosting.

Grease, do not oil, a 9x13-inch pan. In large bowl, mix flour, sugar, coconut, soda, cinnamon, salt, carrots, oil, vanilla, eggs, orange zest, and oranges at medium speed until well blended. Increase to high speed and beat for 2 minutes more. Pour into pan and bake in preheated 350°F oven for 40 to 55 minutes. Remove from oven and cool.

While cake cools, make the frosting. Beat together cream cheese, butter, vanilla, and confectioners' sugar until smooth. Spread on cooled cake and sprinkle with nuts.

Yield: 20 servings.

Donna Bosco
Verona, Pennsylvania

Kiss-Me Cake

&

6 ounces orange juice
concentrate, thawed
1 cup sugar
1 teaspoon salt
½ cup milk
1 cup seedless dark raisins
2 cups unbleached
all-purpose flour
1 teaspoon baking soda
½ cup shortening
2 eggs
⅓ cup chopped walnuts

TOPPING
⅓ cup sugar
1 teaspoon cinnamon
¼ cup chopped walnuts

This recipe has been handed down from my grandmother to my mother and now to me. This unique cake, with its soft texture and orange-cinnamon flavor, can be served anytime—from mid-morning coffee break to late-evening dessert.

In large bowl, combine ½ cup of the concentrate, sugar, salt, milk, raisins, flour, soda, shortening, eggs, and nuts. Blend until all ingredients are moistened, then beat for 3 minutes. Pour into greased and floured 9x13-inch pan and bake in preheated 350°F oven for 35 to 45 minutes, or until a toothpick inserted in the center comes out clean. Let cool 15 minutes in the pan.

Combine topping ingredients in small bowl. Drizzle remaining orange juice concentrate over the warm cake and sprinkle with topping.

Yield: 12 to 16 servings.

*Catherine B. Boyle
Watkins Glen, New York*

PRUNE CAKE

❧

1½ cups sugar

⅔ cup shortening

2 eggs

2 cups unbleached
  all-purpose flour

½ teaspoon salt

1 teaspoon baking soda

1 teaspoon nutmeg

1 teaspoon cinnamon

1 teaspoon cloves

1 cup prune juice

1½ cups chopped, stewed
  prunes

This was the favored birthday cake when I was growing up—a recipe passed along from Great-gramma Esther Foss. We sometimes had sticky white frosting with chopped raisins on it, too, though it is fine with no frosting at all.

Cream together sugar and shortening. Add eggs, one at a time, beating until well blended. In separate bowl, sift flour, salt, soda, and spices. Add alternately with prune juice to the creamed mixture. Stir in chopped prunes.

Pour into greased and floured 10-inch bundt pan and bake in preheated 350°F oven for 50 to 60 minutes, or until tests done.

Yield: 12 servings.

*Mary Jirik
West Rutland, Vermont*

UNCON-VENTIONAL FRUITCAKE

❧

¼ pound (1 stick) butter,
  softened

½ cup oil

4 eggs, slightly beaten

6 large ripe bananas, mashed

2 cups seedless raisins

3 cups unbleached all-purpose
  flour

2½ teaspoons cinnamon

1½ teaspoons cloves

2 teaspoons baking soda

½ teaspoon salt

2 cups sugar

3½ cups coarsely chopped walnuts

This is a special treat to my family because we don't care for the candied fruit that is used in most holiday fruitcakes. Makes a great gift that anyone will enjoy.

Beat together butter, oil, eggs, and bananas. Roll raisins in 1 cup of the flour and set aside. Sift together remaining flour, spices, soda, salt, and sugar, add to wet ingredients, and mix well. Combine flour-coated raisins and walnuts, and stir into batter. Pour into 10-inch tube pan and bake in preheated 350°F oven on middle rack for 1 hour and 45 minutes, or until toothpick comes out clean.

Yield: 12 to 16 servings.

*Dee Ade
Bunnell, Florida*

GRAMMA FREDA'S OATMEAL CAKE

❧

1 cup quick-cooking oats
1½ cups boiling water
½ cup (1 stick) butter, softened
1 cup granulated sugar
1 cup firmly packed brown sugar
2 eggs
2 cups unbleached
  all-purpose flour
½ teaspoon salt
1 teaspoon baking soda
1½ teaspoons cinnamon

TOPPING
6 tablespoons butter
¼ cup brown sugar
½ cup granulated sugar
¼ teaspoon vanilla
¼ cup milk
1 cup chopped walnuts
1 cup shredded coconut

"A classic recipe everybody should have," reported one of our testers, "and it makes a special treat for family or guests, or for a potluck or church supper." The cake is moist and spicy, and the topping is like candy.

In small bowl, combine oats and boiling water, mixing well. In large bowl, cream together butter and sugars, then add eggs and beat until mixture is light and fluffy. Stir in oats mixture, flour, salt, soda, and cinnamon, blending well. Pour into greased 9x13-inch pan and bake in preheated 350°F oven for 30 to 35 minutes.

As soon as cake is done combine topping ingredients in saucepan and heat until bubbly. Spread over top of cake and broil for about 3 minutes, watching carefully to make sure it doesn't burn.

Yield: 12 servings.

Linda Heller
Slippery Rock, Pennsylvania

POUND CAKE

❧

7 eggs
1 pound (2 cups) sugar
1 tablespoon vanilla
1 pound (4 sticks) butter, softened
1 pound (2 cups) unbleached
  all-purpose flour

This recipe (from the Hundley and Otto families) is very special, as it has been made by the family for at least 100 years. It is always included at Christmas with fruitcake and cookies. It stays moist for a long time, freezes well, and is delicious with chocolate sauce or fruit, or lightly toasted.

In medium-size bowl, lightly beat eggs. Sift in sugar and mix thoroughly. Stir in vanilla. In another, larger bowl, beat butter until smooth, then sift in flour, beating thoroughly. Add egg-sugar mixture and stir until well blended. Pour into generously buttered 10-inch tube pan and bake in preheated 325°F oven for 1 hour and 20 minutes. Cool slightly and remove from pan.

Yield: 16 to 20 servings.

Lucy F. Otto
Baltimore, Maryland

Basil Pound Cake

ès

½ pound (2 sticks) butter, softened
2 cups sugar
4 eggs
2 cups unbleached
   all-purpose flour
¼ teaspoon salt
½ teaspoon dried basil leaves

This cake has the wonderful texture of pound cake and the surprising spicy flavor of basil. Since there are more than 50 varieties of basil, the flavor can be changed as you wish. Licorice, lemon, or cinnamon basil make interesting variations. Serve this with hot tea on wintry afternoons, with cool drinks on sultry summer days, or as dessert after any Italian dinner.

In large bowl, cream butter and sugar until light. Beat in eggs, one at a time. Sift flour and salt together in separate bowl, add basil, and stir to combine. Beat into butter mixture until well blended. Pour into greased, 9-inch loaf pan and bake in preheated 300°F oven for 1½ hours, or until cake tests done.

Yield: One 9-inch loaf.

Nancy Leonard
Oklawaha, Florida

GRANDMAMA STROUSE'S COCONUT CREAM CAKE

¾ cup (1½ sticks) butter,
    softened
2 cups sugar
3 eggs, separated
3 cups cake flour
2 teaspoons baking powder
1 teaspoon vanilla
1 cup milk

COCONUT CREAM FILLING
2 cups milk
1 egg, separated
½ cup sugar
3 tablespoons cornstarch
2 cups shredded coconut
1 teaspoon vanilla

This is a very old recipe that belonged to my grandmother's mother. My grandmother always made it for my birthday, and if she were alive today, she'd be 110 years old. Grandmama would mix this in a crock with a wooden spoon, and we would help her with the beating — 150 strokes to cream the butter and sugar, 75 strokes to blend the eggs, 50 strokes to mix the flour and milk, and so forth. The texture was just as fine as that produced by an electric mixer today.

In large bowl, cream butter until light and fluffy. Gradually add sugar and continue beating until fluffy. Add egg yolks and blend well.

Mix flour with baking powder. Stir vanilla into milk and add alternately with flour mixture to creamed butter and sugar, starting and ending with flour.

Beat egg whites and fold gently into batter until no streaks show. Pour into two 9-inch or three 8-inch greased and floured cake pans. Bake in preheated 350°F oven for 25 to 35 minutes, or until cake pulls away from sides of pan. Cool completely on racks.

Meanwhile, make the filling. Scald milk in heavy-bottomed saucepan. Beat egg yolk and add to scalded milk along with sugar and cornstarch. Cook slowly until thick. Add 1 cup of the coconut and the vanilla, stirring to blend. Remove from heat. In separate bowl, beat egg white until stiff and fold into filling. Set aside to cool.

Spread filling between layers and on sides of cooled cake. Sprinkle remaining coconut on top and sides.

Yield: 10 to 12 servings.

Imogene Birchfield
Frankfort, Ohio

DATE CAKE WITH CHOCO-NUT TOPPING

ৰ

1 cup hot water
1 package (6½ ounces) dates,
    finely chopped (about 1¼ cups)
¼ cup shortening
1 cup sugar
1 egg
1 teaspoon vanilla
1⅔ cups sifted unbleached
    all-purpose flour
1 teaspoon baking soda
½ teaspoon salt
½ cup chopped nuts

CHOCO-NUT TOPPING

½ cup semi-sweet
    chocolate chips
2 tablespoons sugar
½ cup finely chopped nuts

Very sweet, moist, and chewy. An all-purpose dessert.

Pour hot water over dates and set aside to cool. Combine shortening, sugar, egg, and vanilla in mixing bowl. Beat 5 minutes, or until fluffy. Sift together flour, soda, and salt. To the creamed mixture, add sifted ingredients alternately with dates and liquid in 4 additions, beginning and ending with dry ingredients. Blend just until smooth, then stir in nuts. Pour into greased and floured 9-inch square pan.

For the topping, combine chocolate chips, sugar, and nuts and sprinkle over batter. Bake in preheated 350°F oven for 45 to 55 minutes.

Yield: 9 servings.

Shirley Virnig
Minneiska, Minnesota

Twenty-Minute Fudge Cake

ॐ

1 stick butter or margarine
½ cup shortening
1 cup water
4 tablespoons cocoa
2 cups sugar
2 cups unbleached
  all-purpose flour
1 teaspoon cinnamon
Pinch of salt
½ cup buttermilk
1 teaspoon baking soda
2 eggs

ICING
1 stick butter or margarine
6 tablespoons milk
4 tablespoons cocoa
Pinch of salt
1 box (1 pound)
  confectioners' sugar
1 teaspoon vanilla
1 cup chopped or whole pecans

I don't remember where I got this recipe, but I've used it for at least 30 years. When my kids were growing up, this was the birthday cake of choice. I'd also have it on hand whenever they came home during college. It's so quick and easy to prepare that it can be made on the spur of the moment for any occasion — and, other than the pan it's baked in, it requires only one pot, which makes for a quick clean-up. The icing tastes like fudge, and the cake itself is equally delicious.

Place butter, shortening, water, and cocoa in large, heavy-bottomed pot and bring to a boil, stirring constantly until thoroughly blended. Remove from heat and stir until mixture no longer bubbles. Sift in sugar, flour, cinnamon, and salt, beating well. Add buttermilk, soda, and eggs, and stir to blend. Pour into greased and floured 10x15-inch jelly-roll pan and bake in preheated 400°F oven for 20 minutes.

Remove cake from oven and make icing in same heavy-bottomed pot. Combine butter, milk, cocoa, and salt, and bring to a boil, stirring constantly. Remove from heat and stir until mixture no longer bubbles. Sift in confectioners' sugar, blending well. Stir in vanilla and nuts, if using chopped nuts. Spread warm icing on cooled cake. Decorate with whole pecans, if using.

Yield: 16 to 18 servings.

Dolly Pearson
Colorado Springs, Colorado

OATMEAL CHOCOLATE CAKE

🍃

1 cup boiling water
½ cup quick-cooking oats
1 teaspoon baking soda
½ cup (1 stick) margarine, softened
1½ cups brown sugar
2 eggs
1 teaspoon vanilla
1 cup unbleached
  all-purpose flour
1 teaspoon baking powder
6 tablespoons cocoa
½ teaspoon salt

This recipe was passed down to me from my great-aunt who lived on Cape Cod near Falmouth, Massachusetts. She said it had been in her family since they came over from England. Her father was a sea captain in the whaling days of New England, and she was one of 14 children. The recipe is a great way to use leftover oatmeal, but I've adapted it for quick-cooking oats. Originally, the cake was wrapped in cheesecloth and could be kept for weeks unrefrigerated. I've never tested that, however, for it's always eaten up soon after it's made.

In small bowl, pour boiling water over oats and soda. Stir and set aside.

In large bowl, cream margarine. Beat in brown sugar, then eggs, one at a time. Add vanilla.

Combine flour, baking powder, cocoa, and salt in separate bowl. Add alternately with oats mixture to eggs and sugar. Pour into greased 8-inch square pan and bake in preheated 350°F oven for 30 to 35 minutes.

Yield: 12 to 16 servings.

B. Weinheimer
Gainesville, Missouri

CHOCOLATE CAKE WITH FLUFFY COCONUT FROSTING

❧

1¾ cups unbleached
　all-purpose flour
2 cups sugar
¾ cup cocoa
1½ teaspoons baking powder
1½ teaspoons baking soda
¾ teaspoon salt
2 eggs
1 cup milk
½ cup oil
2 teaspoons vanilla
1 cup boiling water

FLUFFY
COCONUT FROSTING
1½ cups sugar
2 egg whites
1 tablespoon light corn syrup
1½ teaspoons vanilla
½ teaspoon orange extract
½ teaspoon almond extract
¼ teaspoon salt
½ cup water
1 cup shredded coconut

Very attractive and professional-looking (see page 131)—a moist, light, and chocolaty cake highlighted by a tasty coconut frosting with an unusual combination of orange and almond flavors.

Combine flour, sugar, cocoa, baking powder, soda, and salt in large mixer bowl. Add eggs, milk, oil, and vanilla. Beat 2 minutes at medium speed. At lowest speed, mix in boiling water (batter will be thin). Pour into 2 greased and floured 8-inch round glass baking pans. Bake in preheated 350°F oven for 20 to 30 minutes, or until cake tester inserted in center comes out clean. Cool in pans.

Meanwhile, make the frosting. In top of double boiler, with mixer at high speed, beat all ingredients except coconut until blended, about 1 minute. Place over rapidly boiling water; beat at high speed until soft peaks form (this may take 7 to 8 minutes). Pour into large mixer bowl and beat until thick enough to spread. When cake is completely cooled, spread frosting between layers and on top and sides. Sprinkle coconut on top and press onto sides of cake.

Yield: 16 to 20 servings.

Kathy Durbin
Owaneco, Illinois

ALMOND CHOCOLATE TORTE

❧

2 cups finely ground
  blanched almonds
9 ounces (1½ cups) semi-sweet
  chocolate chips
¼ cup (½ stick) butter
6 eggs, beaten
¾ cup sugar
Pinch of salt
2 tablespoons unbleached
  all-purpose flour
¼ cup brandy or 2 teaspoons
  brandy extract

GLAZE
6 tablespoons water
3 tablespoons sugar
3 ounces (½ cup) semi-sweet
  chocolate chips
1 tablespoon brandy or
  1 teaspoon brandy extract
Whole or split almonds or
  cherries (optional)

This incredibly decadent chocolate dessert freezes beautifully. Slice the torte into servings, wrap individually, and freeze. Then you'll have a very special offering for guests at any time—if you can resist it yourself!

Generously butter 9-inch cake or pie pan and sprinkle with 2 tablespoons of the ground almonds. In double boiler or heavy-bottomed pot, melt chocolate and butter, stirring to blend. Remove from heat.

In large bowl, beat eggs with sugar and salt. Add flour, all but 3 tablespoons of remaining almonds, brandy, and cooled melted chocolate mixture, stirring until thoroughly blended. Bake in preheated 350°F oven for 25 minutes, or until toothpick inserted comes out almost clean. Place on rack and cool partially before inverting; cool completely before transferring from rack to plate.

Meanwhile, make the glaze. Simmer water and sugar in small saucepan until sugar dissolves and mixture has syrupy consistency. Add chocolate and brandy. Heat, stirring, until chocolate melts and glaze coats back of spoon. Drizzle glaze over top of completely cooled torte and decorate with whole or split almonds or cherries, if using.

Yield: 12 to 14 servings.

Cassandra Reeves
Auburn, California

GRANDMA NELSON'S CAKE

20

1½ cups self-rising cake flour
(or 1½ cups cake flour,
1 rounded teaspoon
baking powder, and
½ teaspoon salt)
1 cup sugar
½ cup (1 stick) butter
or margarine, softened
2 eggs, separated
1 teaspoon vanilla
½ cup milk

COFFEE FILLING

3 tablespoons ground coffee
(not instant)
1 cup cold water
1 cup sugar
3 tablespoons cornstarch
¼ cup water
Pinch of salt
1 cup whipping cream

When I want to serve something different and really WOW people, this is what I make. My mother got the recipe when she was first married, but I've never had it anywhere else but home.

Preheat oven to 350°F. Butter bottoms of three 8-inch cake pans. (Use cake pans that have removable bottoms, or use regular pans and line the bottoms with parchment, then butter the parchment.)

Sift flour twice and set aside. In large bowl, cream sugar and butter until light and fluffy. Add egg yolks and vanilla, and beat well. In small bowl, beat egg whites until stiff and set aside. Alternately add milk and flour to butter-and-yolks mixture, beating after each addition. Gently fold egg whites into batter and pour into prepared pans.

Bake for about 15 minutes, just until cake is golden around the edges and begins to pull away from sides of pan; do not overbake or cake will be dry. Remove to racks and cool.

Meanwhile, make the filling. Place coffee and 1 cup cold water in saucepan. Bring to a boil, then strain into a clean saucepan. (You can use the same proportions to make coffee in a coffeemaker, if desired.) Add sugar and bring to a slow boil until sugar is dissolved. Mix cornstarch with ¼ cup water until smooth. Stir into coffee mixture and keep stirring until thickened. Remove from heat and add salt. Set saucepan in bowl of ice and keep stirring so mixture won't lump. Cool completely.

Beat whipping cream until very thick, then fold in cooled coffee mixture. Spread between layers and on top of the cooled cake, but not on sides.

Yield: 12 servings.

Katharyn Risley Hoke
Elkins, New Hampshire

Apricot Pastry Hearts (page 83).

Blueberry Coffee Cake (page 63).

Chiffon Cake (page 32).

Mrs. L's Buttermilk Biscuits (page 120).

Company Pie, top tier, (page 16) and Pear Pie (page 14).

Whole-Wheat Bread (page 171) and Easy Sesame Breadsticks (page 124).

Mexican Corn Bread (page 169).

55

Sugarless Apple Pie (page 11).

Golden Delicious Apple Cake

❧

1 cup unbleached
   all-purpose flour
1 teaspoon baking soda
½ teaspoon salt
¾ pound Golden Delicious
   apples (about 4), peeled,
   cored, and diced
1 egg, beaten
1 cup sugar
½ cup coarsely chopped walnuts
¼ cup oil
1 teaspoon cinnamon
½ teaspoon nutmeg

This is best served the same day it's baked. A hearty cake, it's especially suited for a fall or winter day after a supper of soup or stew.

Sift flour, soda, and salt into small bowl. Toss apples with egg in large bowl, then add sugar, nuts, oil, cinnamon, and nutmeg. Stir in dry ingredients until just moistened. (Batter will be pasty.) Spread batter in greased 8-inch square pan and bake in preheated 350°F oven for 35 to 40 minutes, or until tester inserted in center comes out clean. Cool in pan for at least 10 minutes.

Yield: 9 to 12 servings.

*Victoria Palmer
Greenfield, Massachusetts*

Prize-Winning Applesauce Cake

❧

2 squares (1 ounce each)
   unsweetened chocolate
½ cup (1 stick) margarine
1 cup sugar
2 eggs
1 cup applesauce
1 teaspoon vanilla
1 cup unbleached
   all-purpose flour
½ teaspoon baking powder
¼ teaspoon baking soda
¼ teaspoon salt
⅓ cup chopped nuts (optional)

This quick and easy cake is just right for a busy family who prefers homemade desserts. It does not need an icing, but a dusting of confectioners' sugar adds a dressy touch.

Melt chocolate and margarine in large saucepan, then cool. Add sugar and beat until mixture is creamy. Beat in eggs, one at a time, then add applesauce and vanilla, and mix well. Sift dry ingredients together and add to chocolate mixture, stirring well. Add nuts, if desired. Pour into greased and floured 9-inch square pan and bake in preheated 350°F oven for 30 to 35 minutes, or until toothpick inserted in center comes out clean. Let cool.

Yield: 9 servings.

*Ann Lutz
Clarksville, Ohio*

APPLESAUCE CAKE WITH CARAMEL ICING

❧

½ cup shortening
2 cups granulated sugar
1 egg, beaten
1½ cups unsweetened applesauce
2 teaspoons baking soda
½ cup boiling water
2½ cups unbleached
  all-purpose flour
½ teaspoon salt
½ teaspoon each of cinnamon,
  cloves, and allspice
1 cup raisins
½ cup chopped walnuts

CARAMEL ICING
1 stick margarine
1 cup brown sugar
½ cup evaporated milk
1 cup granulated sugar

An all-time favorite that can be served with or without the icing. Makes an excellent treat for bake sales, church suppers, or picnics.

Cream together shortening and sugar. Blend in egg and applesauce. In separate bowl, combine soda and boiling water. Sift together flour, salt, cinnamon, cloves, and allspice. To the creamed mixture, add water-and-soda mixture alternately with flour mixture, beginning and ending with flour. Fold raisins and walnuts into batter. Pour into 9x13-inch pan and bake in preheated 350°F oven for 1 hour.

To make the icing, melt margarine and brown sugar in saucepan over low heat. Add evaporated milk and granulated sugar. Boil for 3 minutes and beat well. Spread on cooled cake.

Yield: 20 servings.

Carolyn Albright
Cairo, Missouri

ENGLISH APPLE PUDDING CAKE

❧

1 cup (2 sticks) butter, softened
4 cups sugar
4 eggs
8 large unpeeled apples, cored and chopped
4 cups unbleached all-purpose flour
4 teaspoons cinnamon
1½ teaspoons nutmeg
4 teaspoons baking soda
1 teaspoon salt

SAUCE
½ cup (1 stick) butter
1 cup sugar
1 tablespoon cream
3 tablespoons rum

This makes a large quantity of sauce, so you might want to reduce it by a third, or refrigerate what you don't use and reheat it at another time as a topping for vanilla ice cream.

Cream butter and sugar, then add eggs and beat thoroughly. Stir in apples and mix well.

Sift together flour, cinnamon, nutmeg, soda, and salt, and combine with apple mixture, blending well. Pour into greased 10-inch tube pan and bake in preheated 400°F oven for about 1 hour.

Remove cake to cooling rack and prepare the sauce. In a saucepan, melt butter. Add sugar and cream, and boil for a few minutes, then remove from heat. Stir in rum. Pour over warm cake and serve.

Yield: 12 servings.

Charles R. Sansone
Hillsboro, Ohio

HEARTY APPLE CAKE

❧

3 cups whole-wheat flour
1 teaspoon baking soda
½ teaspoon salt
1 teaspoon cinnamon
2 cups firmly packed
    brown sugar
1¼ cups oil
2 eggs
2 teaspoons vanilla
2 cups peeled, cored, and
    shredded or chopped apples
½ cup chopped nuts
Confectioners' sugar (optional)

A toothsome whole-wheat cake that makes a nutritious snack.

Combine flour, soda, salt, and cinnamon. In separate bowl, beat brown sugar, oil, eggs, and vanilla until light and fluffy. Add flour mixture, stirring until just blended. Mixture will be thick. Fold in apples and nuts. Pour into greased and floured 10-inch bundt pan and bake in preheated 325°F oven for 1 hour, or until top springs back when pressed with finger. Cool in pan for 10 minutes. Remove from pan and allow to cool completely. Sprinkle with confectioners' sugar, if desired.

Yield: 12 servings.

Marjorie DiGregorio
New York, New York

CHOCO-DOT PUMPKIN CAKE

❧

4 eggs
1 can (16 ounces) pumpkin
¾ cup oil
1 cup All-Bran cereal
2 cups unbleached
    all-purpose flour
2 teaspoons baking powder
1 teaspoon baking soda
½ teaspoon salt
1½ teaspoons cinnamon
½ teaspoon cloves
¼ teaspoon ginger
¼ teaspoon nutmeg
¼ teaspoon allspice
2 cups sugar
1 package (6 ounces)
    semi-sweet chocolate chips

This is my husband's favorite cake. It packs well in a lunch box and also makes a great snack accompanied with a glass of ice-cold milk.

In large bowl, beat eggs until foamy. Add pumpkin, oil, and cereal, and mix well. Sift in flour, baking powder, soda, salt, spices, and sugar, and stir to blend. Mix in chocolate chips. Pour batter into greased 10-inch bundt or tube pan and bake in preheated 350°F oven for about 1 hour and 10 minutes. Cool completely before removing from pan. Serve warm or cool.

Yield: 12 servings.

Francine Derus
Westlake, Oregon

PUMPKIN CAKE ROLL

ॐ

¾ cup unbleached
    all-purpose flour
1 teaspoon baking powder
2 teaspoons cinnamon
1 teaspoon ginger
½ teaspoon nutmeg
Dash of salt
3 eggs
1 cup granulated sugar
⅔ cup cooked, mashed pumpkin
1 teaspoon lemon juice
½ cup chopped walnuts
Confectioners' sugar

FILLING
1 package (3 ounces) cream
    cheese, softened
4 tablespoons butter, softened
1 cup confectioners' sugar
½ teaspoon vanilla

Even a beginning baker will have success—and fun—making this cake roll. It's sweet and rich, and an attractive addition to a holiday dinner or party.

Stir together flour, baking powder, cinnamon, ginger, nutmeg, and salt, and set aside. In large bowl, beat eggs until thick, then gradually add granulated sugar, beating until well blended. Stir in pumpkin and lemon juice, mixing thoroughly. Fold in dry ingredients. Spread batter in greased 10 x 15-inch jelly-roll pan and sprinkle with chopped nuts. Bake in preheated 350°F oven for 15 minutes.

Remove cake from oven. Sprinkle top with confectioners' sugar, place a towel over cake, then a cool baking sheet, and invert cake. Remove jelly-roll pan gently and roll cake up in towel to cool.

Meanwhile, make the filling. Beat together cream cheese and butter until fluffy. Add confectioners' sugar and mix until smooth. Stir in vanilla.

After cake cools, carefully unroll it and spread with filling. Roll back up and refrigerate until ready to serve.

Yield: 30 slices.

*Debbie Roberts
Lake City, Minnesota*

GRANNY SMITH COFFEE CAKE

2 cups unbleached
   all-purpose flour
1½ cups sugar
1 teaspoon cinnamon
1 teaspoon baking soda
1 teaspoon salt
1 cup oil
3 eggs
1 teaspoon vanilla
4 small Granny Smith apples,
   peeled, cored, and thinly sliced
¼ cup chopped pecans

STREUSEL TOPPING
½ cup unbleached
   all-purpose flour
¼ cup packed brown sugar
¼ cup margarine
¼ cup chopped pecans

"Best apple cake I've ever had," reported one of our recipe testers. "Lots of apples (be sure to slice them very thin) and a flavorful crunchy topping. This makes a fine breakfast cake, snack, or family dessert."

Preheat oven to 375°F. Grease and flour 10-inch tube pan. Sift together flour, sugar, cinnamon, soda, and salt, and set aside. Beat together oil, eggs, and vanilla. Stir in flour mixture, add apples and pecans, and mix gently. Spread batter in prepared pan.

Combine streusel ingredients, cutting in margarine to a crumblike consistency. Distribute mixture evenly over top of batter and bake for 50 to 55 minutes, or until toothpick comes out clean.

Yield: 12 servings.

Peggy Dombrowski
South Amboy, New Jersey

RHUBARB COFFEE CAKE

1½ cups granulated sugar
½ cup shortening
1 egg
2 cups unbleached
   all-purpose flour
1 teaspoon baking soda
(continued)

A nice change of pace. The rhubarb adds a subtle flavor and keeps the cake moist. For a pretty presentation, bake in a pan with a removable bottom and serve on a fancy platter.

In large bowl, cream together sugar and shortening. Add egg and beat well. In separate bowl, mix together flour, soda, and salt. Add alternately with buttermilk to creamed mixture, then stir in vanilla and rhubarb, mixing well. Pour into greased 9x13-inch pan or 10-inch springform pan.

(continued)

½ teaspoon salt
1 cup buttermilk
1 teaspoon vanilla
1½ cups finely chopped rhubarb

TOPPING
¼ cup granulated sugar
¼ cup brown sugar
1 teaspoon cinnamon

Combine topping ingredients and sprinkle over top of cake batter. Bake in preheated 350°F oven for 35 to 40 minutes, or until it tests done.

Yield: 12 servings.

Dorothy Firchau
Lewisville, Minnesota

BLUEBERRY COFFEE CAKE

 è•

⅓ cup plus 2 tablespoons oil
¾ cup milk
1 egg
½ teaspoon lemon extract
1¾ cups flour (half whole-wheat,
   half unbleached all-purpose)
1 cup sugar
½ teaspoon salt
2½ teaspoons baking powder
2 cups blueberries
   (fresh or frozen)

TOPPING
½ cup chopped nuts
¼ cup brown sugar
½ teaspoon allspice
¼ cup combined flour (as above)

This is frequently requested by my quilting circle—The Wednesday Afternoon Ladies Stitch and Bitch Society— so I generally double the recipe to have plenty for everyone (see page 50).

Beat together ⅓ cup oil, milk, egg, and lemon extract. Mix in flour, sugar, salt, and baking powder, then gently add 1 cup of the blueberries. Pour into greased 9-inch square pan. Mix topping ingredients until blended and sprinkle over batter. Drizzle with last 2 tablespoons oil and add last cup blueberries. Bake in preheated 375°F oven for 45 to 50 minutes.

Yield: 16 servings.

Cindy Tompkins
Creswell, Oregon

BABKA

DOUGH
1 package dry yeast
¼ cup warm water
½ cup sugar
4 cups unbleached
    all-purpose flour
1 cup (2 sticks) butter
1 cup warm milk
3 egg yolks, slightly beaten

FILLING
3 egg whites
2 tablespoons cinnamon
1 cup sugar
1 cup ground walnuts

STREUSEL
6 tablespoons unbleached
    all-purpose flour
2 tablespoons sugar
2 tablespoons butter

This is a relatively easy yeast coffee cake that does not require kneading, and its initial rising is in the refrigerator, so the shaping and final rising can be done at any time the following day. It is delicious and remains moist for several days. A large slice can be reheated by buttering and lightly browning in a skillet—absolutely heavenly.

To make the dough, dissolve yeast in water and set aside. Mix together sugar and flour, then cut in butter, using a pastry blender or two knives. Combine milk, egg yolks, and yeast mixture, and stir into flour and sugar mixture. Cover and refrigerate overnight.

When ready to proceed with recipe, make filling. Beat egg whites until frothy. Add cinnamon, sugar, and walnuts, and beat well.

Divide chilled dough into 4 equal pieces and roll out each on lightly floured surface into 9x12-inch rectangle. Spread each with one-fourth of filling mixture. Starting from the long side, roll up each piece, pinch to seal seam, and press ends of rolls under to seal. Place in greased 10-inch tube pan in two layers, with two rolls per layer. Make sure the top rolls overlap the lower rolls like bricks. Cover and let rise in warm place for 1 hour, or until doubled in bulk.

When dough has risen, make streusel topping. Combine flour and sugar, and cut in butter until mixture has crumbly consistency. Sprinkle on top of dough and bake in preheated 350°F oven for 50 minutes.

Yield: 16 to 20 servings.

Judith Smith
Killingworth, Connecticut

SEASONAL FRUITCAKE

ಜ಄

1 package dry yeast
¼ teaspoon sugar
¼ cup lukewarm water
¾ cup lukewarm milk
Grated zest of 1 lemon
2 large eggs
⅓ cup sugar
3½ to 4 cups sifted
    unbleached all-purpose flour
6 tablespoons butter or
    margarine, softened
6 to 7 medium apples, peeled,
    cored, and sliced

STREUSEL TOPPING
1 cup sifted unbleached
    all-purpose flour
⅔ cup sugar
1 teaspoon cinnamon
½ cup (1 stick)
    well-chilled butter

This German cake was made by my mother throughout the year. Using a yeast-cake base, she varied it with the seasons: apple cake for fall, streusel cake in winter and spring, and blueberry or plum cake in summer.

Sprinkle yeast and ¼ teaspoon sugar over lukewarm water. Let sit 2 to 3 minutes, then stir to dissolve and set in warm, draft-free place for 5 minutes. Mix in lukewarm milk and lemon zest.

In large bowl, beat eggs, then add ⅓ cup sugar, and mix well. Stir in yeast mixture and add flour, 1 cup at a time, mixing well after each addition. Beat in butter, 1 tablespoon at a time. Gather dough into a ball and place on lightly floured surface. Knead for about 10 minutes, until dough is smooth and elastic, adding flour if dough is too moist.

Place in greased bowl, cover with towel, and put in warm, draft-free place for 40 minutes, or until doubled in bulk.

Remove dough to greased baking sheet and roll out or stretch to fill sheet, making the surface smooth and a slight, raised rim around the edge. Arrange apple slices on top of dough in lengthwise, parallel rows.

Make topping by mixing flour, sugar, and cinnamon together. Cut in butter until topping has a coarse, crumbly consistency. Sprinkle over apples. Bake in preheated 350°F oven for 40 to 45 minutes, or until crust is golden brown. Serve warm with ice cream, or cold with whipped cream, or plain.

VARIATIONS
For Plum Cake, replace apples with about 3 pounds pitted, quartered plums, arranged in rows with skin side down. Sprinkle with 1 cup sugar mixed with 1 teaspoon cinnamon and drizzle ¼ cup melted butter evenly over top of dough. Bake as described above.

(continued)

For Streusel Cake, use 2 to 3 cups applesauce instead of sliced apples and spread over surface of dough. Using twice the amount of streusel topping given in main recipe, sprinkle over top and bake as described above.

For Blueberry Cake, brush surface of dough with melted butter and replace apples with 1 to 2 pints blueberries, pressing lightly into the dough. (Try not to get them too close to the edge, for they can burst and drip all over the oven.) Sprinkle with ½ to 1 cup sugar mixed with 1 teaspoon cinnamon and bake as described above.

Yield: 20 to 25 servings.

Susi von Oettingen
Bradford, New Hampshire

FRUIT COFFEE CAKE

ও

1 package dry yeast
2 tablespoons warm water
2 cups unbleached all-purpose flour, sifted
½ cup (1 stick) butter
½ teaspoon salt
2 tablespoons sugar
⅓ cup milk, scalded
1 egg, slightly beaten
Sliced fresh fruit (apples, plums, peaches, or a combination)

TOPPING
2 tablespoons unbleached all-purpose flour
1 cup sugar
¼ cup (½ stick) chilled butter
2 teaspoons cinnamon

My mother-in-law, Florence Vojtisek, gave me this recipe. It is more like pastry than a conventional coffee cake, with rows of apple slices glazed with caramelized sugar.

Dissolve yeast in water and set aside. In large bowl, cut flour and butter to cornmeal consistency. Stir salt and sugar into scalded milk and let cool. Add egg and yeast mixture to cooled milk and stir well. Combine with flour-and-butter mixture. Dough will be sticky and a little difficult to handle. Place in 9x13-inch greased pan and let rise until doubled in bulk. Evenly distribute sliced fruit over top, then let rest 5 minutes. With pastry blender or two knives, cut topping ingredients to a crumbly consistency and sprinkle over fruit. Bake in preheated 350°F oven for 25 to 35 minutes.

Yield: 12 servings.

Louise Vojtisek
Middlebury, Vermont

RASPBERRY CREAM-CHEESE COFFEE CAKE

❧

CRUST
2¼ cups unbleached
   all-purpose flour
¾ cup sugar
¾ cup (1½ sticks)
   margarine, chilled
½ teaspoon baking powder
½ teaspoon baking soda
¼ teaspoon salt
¾ cup sour cream or plain yogurt
1 egg
1 teaspoon almond extract

FILLING
1 package (8 ounces)
   cream cheese, softened
¼ cup sugar
1 egg

TOPPING
½ cup raspberry preserves
½ cup sliced almonds

This recipe has traveled far and wide since my sister-in-law, Kathy George Reading, brought it from Iowa to Ohio for a family reunion. Although it's called a coffee cake, it also would make an elegant dessert. A real show-stopper, it is rich yet delicate in flavor and looks like it requires a lot of work — but it doesn't!

To make the crust, combine flour and sugar in large bowl. Cut in margarine with fork or pastry blender until mixture resembles coarse crumbs. Set aside 1 cup of crumb mixture. To remaining crumb mixture, add baking powder, soda, salt, sour cream, egg, and almond extract. Blend well. Spread batter over bottom and 2 inches up sides of greased and floured 9- or 10-inch springform pan. (Batter should be about ¼-inch thick on sides. If you have difficulty spreading batter up the sides, refrigerate for about 10 minutes to stiffen it.)

Combine the filling ingredients and beat well. Spread over batter in pan.

Carefully spoon preserves evenly over cheese filling. In small bowl, combine reserved crumb mixture with sliced almonds and sprinkle over top.

Bake in preheated 350°F oven for 45 to 55 minutes, or until cream cheese filling is set and crust is deep golden brown. Cool 15 minutes, then remove sides of pan.

Serve warm or cool, cut into wedges. Refrigerate leftovers.

Yield: 12 to 16 servings.

Ann Lutz
Clarksville, Ohio

HUNGARIAN COFFEE CAKE

❧

1 cup hot water
½ cup raisins
1 package (1 tablespoon) dry yeast
1¼ cups lukewarm water
1¼ cups sugar
¾ cup (1½ sticks) butter, melted
½ to 1 teaspoon salt
1 egg, beaten
3½ to 4 cups unbleached
   all-purpose flour
2½ teaspoons cinnamon
½ cup chopped walnuts

This was my grandmother's recipe, and I can still remember helping her make it when I was a child. My dad swears there's nothing better for breakfast or dessert. Enhanced with a sweet raisin swirl, this cake has great taste, great looks, and lots of room for creativity.

In small bowl, pour hot water over raisins and set aside.

Dissolve yeast in warm water. Add ¼ cup of the sugar, ¼ cup of the melted butter (cooled to lukewarm), salt, egg, and 3½ cups flour. Mix until blended.

On floured surface, knead dough until smooth and elastic, adding more flour if needed. Let rise until doubled in bulk, punch down, and form dough into balls the size of walnuts. Dip in remaining ½ cup melted butter, then roll in a mixture of remaining 1 cup sugar, cinnamon, and walnuts.

Using a well-greased solid-bottom 10-inch tube pan, place half the balls in 2 rings in the bottom. Drain raisins, pat dry, and distribute over the first layer. Repeat with remaining balls. Let rise to the top of the pan and bake in preheated 350°F oven for 35 to 40 minutes. Run a knife around edges to loosen, then turn out onto serving plate.

Yield: 16 to 18 servings.

Carrie Ringer
Quinter, Kansas

REFRIGERATOR COFFEE CAKE

ॐ

1 package dry yeast
1 cup lukewarm milk
1 cup shortening
4 cups unbleached
   all-purpose flour
   (possibly more)
3 tablespoons sugar
1 teaspoon salt
3 eggs, beaten
2 tablespoons butter, melted

NUT FILLING
½ cup brown sugar
4 teaspoons cinnamon
1 cup ground walnuts
   (or ½ cup walnuts and
   ½ cup raisins)

CHEESE FILLING
2 packages (8 ounces each)
   cream cheese, softened
½ cup sugar
4 egg yolks
4 tablespoons unbleached
   all-purpose flour

FROSTING
1 cup confectioners' sugar
Water

Beautiful and delicious. Serve for brunch or give as a holiday gift or special thank-you present.

Stir yeast into milk and set aside to soften. Cut shortening into flour until mixture is crumbly. Add sugar, salt, and eggs to yeast mixture, blend well, and stir into flour mixture. Cover and refrigerate overnight.

Punch down and let rest for 10 minutes. Cut dough in half and roll each half into 11x14-inch rectangle. Brush each half with melted butter.

Combine ingredients for either filling (or prepare half the amount of both) and sprinkle/spread over both rectangles. Starting from the long side, roll up like a jelly roll, pinch seam to seal, and turn ends under. Place on greased baking sheet, seam side down. Cover and let rise in warm place until doubled in bulk. With single-edge razor blade or sharp knife, cut a slit running the length of the roll to within 1 inch of each end, cutting through top two layers. Bake in preheated 350°F oven for 20 minutes.

For the frosting, combine confectioners' sugar with enough water for desired consistency and drizzle over top of coffee cake while still warm.

Yield: 2 coffee cakes, 10 to 12 servings each.

Judith A. Smith
Killingworth, Connecticut

COOKIES
& BARS

ANNE'S OATMEAL COOKIES

ə♣

3 sticks butter, softened
   (or half butter, half margarine)
1 cup brown sugar
1 egg
1 tablespoon vanilla
2½ cups oats
2 cups unbleached
   all-purpose flour
½ teaspoon salt
1 cup raisins
1 cup chopped nuts (optional)
⅔ cup strawberry preserves
   (or your preference)

When I send a "care package" of cookies to my son Richard, who lives in New Hampshire, I always include these. They travel well and make a nutritious snack. (See page 134.)

Cream butter and brown sugar until fluffy. Add egg and vanilla, and beat well. In separate bowl, combine oats, flour, salt, raisins, and nuts, if using. Stir into sugar mixture and blend thoroughly. Roll dough into 1-inch balls and place on ungreased cookie sheets. Flatten slightly and make a depression on top with your thumb. Fill each dent with small amount of preserves and bake in preheated 350°F oven for 8 to 10 minutes with one cookie sheet on top shelf of oven and the other on bottom shelf. Reverse sheets and bake 8 to 10 minutes longer.

Yield: 4 dozen.

Anne Pisciotta
Huntington, New York

LEMON OATMEAL COOKIES

ə♣

2 sticks margarine, softened
1 cup granulated sugar
½ cup brown sugar
2 eggs
2 teaspoons lemon extract
1 tablespoon mace or nutmeg
1 teaspoon baking soda
4 teaspoons baking powder
½ teaspoon salt
1½ cups whole-wheat flour
3 to 4 cups oats
1 to 1½ cups chopped pecans
1 cup raisins

A subtle lemon flavor makes these hearty cookies distinctive. If the dough seems too crumbly to drop from a spoon, use your fingers to shape it into mounds or balls, then flatten each slightly before baking.

Cream margarine and sugars, then add eggs and lemon extract, beating well. Stir in mace, soda, baking powder, salt, flour, oats, pecans, and raisins, and blend thoroughly. Place teaspoonfuls of dough on ungreased cookie sheets and press slightly, since the dough is stiff. Bake in preheated 350°F oven for 9 minutes. Cool on wire racks.

Yield: 4 dozen.

Sylvester Allred
Flagstaff, Arizona

TEXAS BUFFALO CHIPS

੨ф

2 cups (4 sticks) butter, softened
2 cups granulated sugar
2 cups brown sugar
4 eggs
2 teaspoons vanilla
4 cups whole-wheat flour
4 cups rolled oats (processed to a powder in blender)
1 teaspoon salt
2 teaspoons baking soda
1 package (12 ounces) milk chocolate chips
3 cups chopped pecans

Typical of the Lone Star State, these cookies are big—in size, appeal, and yield. The recipe makes enough to feed an army—or at least a few hungry kids.

Cream butter and sugars together. Add eggs and vanilla, and beat well. Combine flour, oats, salt, and soda, and mix thoroughly with creamed ingredients. Stir in chocolate chips and pecans. Roll dough into 2-inch balls and place 2 inches apart on ungreased cookie sheets. Bake in preheated 350°F oven for 8 to 10 minutes, or until browned. Let cool for a few minutes before removing from cookie sheet.

Yield: 6½ dozen.

Stan Shawhart
Arthur City, Texas

GRANDMA'S COOKIES

੨ф

3 sticks margarine, softened
1 cup brown sugar
1 cup granulated sugar
2 eggs, slightly beaten
1 teaspoon vanilla
2 heaping cups unbleached all-purpose flour
1 teaspoon baking powder
1 teaspoon baking soda
1 teaspoon salt
2 cups quick-cooking oats
2 cups Rice Krispies cereal
2 cups semi-sweet chocolate chips
½ to ¾ cup chopped nuts (optional)

We never visit Grandma without leaving with a bag of these in our hands! They are a wonderful variation of the basic chocolate-chip cookie, and everyone who tastes them for the first time instantly loves them.

Cream together margarine and sugars. Add eggs and vanilla, and beat well. Sift together flour, baking powder, soda, and salt, and add to egg mixture, mixing thoroughly. Stir in oats, Rice Krispies, chocolate chips, and nuts, if using. Drop by teaspoonfuls onto greased cookie sheets. Bake in preheated 350°F oven for 10 minutes.

Yield: 5 dozen.

Cyndi Hale
Northville, Michigan

MAGIC PEANUT BUTTER MIDDLES

❧

COOKIE DOUGH
1½ cups unbleached
   all-purpose flour
½ cup cocoa
½ teaspoon baking soda
½ cup granulated sugar
½ cup firmly packed brown sugar
½ cup (1 stick) margarine,
   softened
¼ cup peanut butter
1 teaspoon vanilla
1 egg

FILLING
¾ cup peanut butter
¾ cup confectioners' sugar

Sparkly topped cookies with a wonderful explosion of peanut butter and chocolate. Be careful not to overbake these, because they harden as they cool and can become too hard if baked longer than suggested.

In small bowl, combine flour, cocoa, and soda, blending well. In large bowl, beat sugars, margarine, and ¼ cup peanut butter until light and fluffy. Add vanilla and egg, and beat well. Stir in flour mixture until blended and set aside.

In another small bowl, combine filling ingredients and blend thoroughly. Roll into thirty 1-inch balls.

With floured hands, shape about 1 tablespoonful of dough around 1 peanut butter ball, covering completely. Place 2 inches apart on ungreased cookie sheets. Flatten with bottom of glass dipped in sugar. Bake in preheated 375°F oven for 7 to 9 minutes, or until set and slightly cracked. Cool on wire racks.

Yield: 2½ to 3 dozen.

Patricia Kerecz
La Habra, California

FAMOUS PEANUT BUTTER COOKIES

❧

1 cup shortening
1 cup granulated sugar
1 cup brown sugar
2 eggs
1 teaspoon vanilla
1 cup creamy peanut butter
3 cups unbleached
   all-purpose flour
2 teaspoons baking soda
½ teaspoon salt (optional)
1 cup chopped peanuts

Equally appealing to adults and children. Depending on the saltiness of the peanut butter and peanuts used, you may want to eliminate the salt altogether.

Cream together shortening, sugars, eggs, and vanilla. Stir in peanut butter until well blended. Sift dry ingredients together, then stir into creamed mixture. Add peanuts and mix well. Roll dough into balls and place on ungreased cookie sheets. Press down with floured fork to make criss-cross pattern. Bake in preheated 350°F oven for 10 minutes, or until done.

Yield: 3 to 4 dozen.

*Lisa Crouch
San Jose, California*

EASY PEANUT BUTTER COOKIES

❧

1 cup chunky peanut butter
1 cup granulated sugar
1 egg, beaten
½ teaspoon vanilla

There are only four ingredients in this recipe, which cuts down on utensils used as well as time. The cookies tend to become harder the longer they bake, so you might want to experiment with the first batch or two to determine the texture you prefer.

Mix peanut butter and sugar together, blending well. Stir in egg and vanilla. Shape into 1-inch balls and place on ungreased cookie sheets. Press with fork to flatten slightly. Bake in preheated 350°F oven for 12 to 15 minutes. (Shorter baking time will yield softer cookies.) Cool on wire rack.

Yield: 2 dozen.

*Debbie Dawson
Riverside, California*

ALMOND BUTTER COOKIES

੨੭

1 cup (2 sticks) butter, softened
3 tablespoons sugar
1 teaspoon almond extract
2 cups sifted unbleached all-purpose flour
¼ teaspoon salt

FROSTING
1 cup confectioners' sugar
1 tablespoon butter, softened
½ teaspoon vanilla
2 tablespoons hot water (approximately)
Unblanched sliced almonds

I make these light and delicate cookies every Christmas because they are so well received. They should not be overbaked, so remove them from the oven just as the sides start to turn golden.

In large mixing bowl, cream butter thoroughly. Add sugar and almond extract and beat well. Sift together flour and salt, gradually add to creamed mixture, and stir until thoroughly blended. Chill dough for ease in handling.

Shape into 1-inch balls, place on cookie sheets, and flatten to ¼-inch thickness with bottom of glass dipped in flour. Bake in preheated 350°F oven for 10 to 12 minutes.

While cookies are cooling, make frosting. In small bowl, beat together confectioners' sugar, butter, vanilla, and enough hot water to give a smooth consistency. Spread about ½ teaspoon frosting on each cookie and decorate with one sliced almond.

Yield: 3 dozen.

Donna Bosco
Verona, Pennsylvania

OATMEAL-RAISIN CHOCOLATE-CHIP COOKIES

ða

¾ cup (1½ sticks) butter, softened
1 cup granulated sugar
1 tablespoon dark brown sugar
1 egg, beaten
¼ cup molasses
2 tablespoons water
1½ cups unbleached
   all-purpose flour
1 teaspoon baking soda
¼ teaspoon ginger
1 teaspoon cinnamon
1 cup quick-cooking oats
¾ cup chopped walnuts
½ cup plumped white raisins
¾ cup semi-sweet chocolate chips

These delightful, wholesome, quick-and-easy cookies are great for a lunch-box treat or after-school snack. Plumping the raisins (boiling them in water to cover for just a couple of minutes, then draining) gives softness to the cookie texture.

Cream butter and sugars. Add egg, molasses, and water, and blend well. Sift in flour, soda, and spices, and mix thoroughly. Stir in oats, nuts, raisins, and chocolate chips. (Batter will be stiff.)

Drop by spoonfuls onto ungreased cookie sheets and bake in preheated 325°F oven for 9 to 10 minutes, or until nicely browned on top.

Yield: 4 dozen.

*John Craig
Easthampton, Massachusetts*

SPICY OATMEAL & CHOCOLATE-CHIP COOKIES

ঌ

1 cup (2 sticks) margarine
  or butter, softened
2 cups brown sugar
2 cups unbleached
  all-purpose flour
2 cups rolled oats
1 teaspoon baking soda
½ teaspoon salt
1 tablespoon cinnamon
1 teaspoon nutmeg
½ teaspoon cloves
2 eggs
1 tablespoon vanilla
2 tablespoons milk
¾ cup chopped pecans or
  walnuts
1 package (6 ounces)
  semi-sweet chocolate chips

An excellent cookie enlivened with spices. These are a snap to make and are ready in no time.

Cream together margarine and brown sugar. Stir in flour, oats, soda, salt, cinnamon, nutmeg, and cloves, and mix well. In separate bowl, beat together eggs, vanilla, and milk. Add to oats mixture and blend thoroughly. Stir in nuts and chocolate chips.

Drop by spoonfuls onto ungreased cookie sheets. Bake in preheated 350°F oven for 10 to 12 minutes, or until lightly browned. Cool on racks.

Yield: 4 dozen.

Kelly A. Murphy
Natchez, Mississippi

PISTACHIO ICEBOX COOKIES

ﻌ

½ cup (1 stick) butter or margarine, softened
1 cup sugar
1 egg
1 teaspoon vanilla
1½ cups unbleached all-purpose flour
½ teaspoon baking powder
½ cup chopped pistachios

Pistachios give these cookies a unique taste and appearance. They are light and crisp, and convenient to have on hand. When you make them, prepare an extra batch, seal the log-shaped dough in plastic wrap, and store in the freezer until needed.

Cream butter and sugar thoroughly, then beat in egg and vanilla. Combine flour and baking powder, and add to creamed mixture, blending well. Stir in nuts. Shape dough into two log-shaped rolls about 1¼ inches in diameter. Wrap in wax paper and chill thoroughly.

Cut into ¼-inch-thick slices and bake in preheated 400°F oven for 6 to 7 minutes, or until barely browned on edges.

Yield: About 6 dozen.

Dorothy Firchau
Lewisville, Minnesota

PECAN PRALINE COOKIES

ﻌ

1⅔ cups sifted unbleached all-purpose flour
1½ teaspoons baking powder
½ teaspoon salt
½ cup (1 stick) butter or margarine, softened
1½ cups packed brown sugar
1 egg
1 teaspoon vanilla
1 cup pecan halves
(continued)

Special enough to serve at a party or to give as a gift. Because the batter spreads while baking, be sure to leave adequate space between each one on the cookie sheet.

Sift flour with baking powder and salt, and set aside. In large bowl, cream butter, then add brown sugar gradually, beating well. Blend in egg, vanilla, and reserved dry ingredients, mixing thoroughly. Drop by rounded teaspoonfuls about 2 inches apart onto ungreased cookie sheets. Bake in preheated 350°F oven for 10 minutes.

While cookies are cooling, break pecan halves into 2 to 4 pieces. Make the frosting by combining brown sugar and cream in small saucepan. Bring to boil, stirring constantly, and boil 2 minutes. Remove from heat, blend in confectioners' sugar, and beat until smooth. If frosting thickens,

FROSTING
1 cup packed brown sugar
½ cup cream
1 cup sifted
  confectioners' sugar

thin with additional cream. Place 4 or 5 pecan pieces on each cookie, then drizzle a teaspoonful of frosting over top.

Yield: 5 dozen.

Mary Glynn Johnson
Wytheville, Virginia

CATTERN CAKES

2 cups unbleached
  all-purpose flour
2 teaspoons baking powder
¼ cup currants
½ cup ground almonds
2 teaspoons anise seeds
1 cup sugar
½ teaspoon cinnamon
10 tablespoons butter or
  margarine, melted
1 egg, beaten

These cakes are also known as Catherine Wheels, after St. Catherine, who was martyred in A.D. 310 and is the patron saint of maidens and lacemakers. My recipe is from a British lady whose "afternoon tea" included typical sandwiches and baked goods. Originally, the recipe called for caraway seeds, but I've made it both ways and prefer the anise seeds. These are perfect with fresh-brewed tea. (Our recipe tester rated them as one of the best cookies she had tasted in years, and her husband liked them so much he didn't want her to take any to work!)

Mix together flour, baking powder, currants, almonds, anise seeds, sugar, and cinnamon. Add cooled melted butter and egg, and stir to form a soft dough. Pinch off walnut-size pieces, roll into balls, and place on ungreased cookie sheets. Flatten with fork to make crisscross pattern and bake in preheated 400°F oven for 10 to 12 minutes, or until lightly browned. Cool on wire rack.

Yield: 2½ dozen.

Ingrid J. Apel
Ann Arbor, Michigan

CRYBABY COOKIES

ﾆ

1 cup raisins
4 cups unbleached
  all-purpose flour
1 cup sugar
2 tablespoons shortening
2 eggs, beaten
1 cup molasses
1 cup milk
2 teaspoons baking soda
1 teaspoon salt
1 teaspoon cinnamon
½ teaspoon each nutmeg,
  cloves, and allspice
¼ teaspoon ginger

Absolutely delicious—almost like spice cake. Kids love them, they keep well, and they're not expensive. The recipe makes a large quantity, too.

Toss raisins with a small amount of the flour and set aside. Cream sugar and shortening until light, then add eggs, molasses, and milk, beating well. Sift together remaining flour, soda, salt, and spices, and add gradually to creamed mixture, stirring to blend. Mix in floured raisins.

Drop by teaspoonfuls onto greased cookie sheets and bake in preheated 325 to 350°F oven for 10 to 12 minutes.

Yield: 6 dozen.

Eba Babcock
Mannsville, New York

SURPRISE COOKIES

ﾆ

1 cup granulated sugar
1½ cups brown sugar
1 cup shortening
3 eggs
1 teaspoon vanilla
7 cups unbleached
  all-purpose flour
1 cup light molasses
1 pound raisins
¼ cup boiling water
2 teaspoons baking soda
1 egg, beaten

Ground raisins give these cookies a soft and chewy texture, and brushing the tops with a beaten egg creates an appealing, shiny appearance.

In large bowl, cream sugars and shortening together until light. Add eggs and vanilla, and beat well. Stir in flour and molasses, mixing until thoroughly blended.

Pour raisins and boiling water into blender or food processor and grind. Add soda and pulse to mix. Stir raisin mixture into cookie dough, which should be very stiff at this point. Roll into walnut-size balls and place on greased cookie sheets. Press down slightly and brush tops with beaten egg. Bake in preheated 350°F oven for 12 to 15 minutes.

Yield: 8 to 8½ dozen.

Dorothy Swinehart
West Salem, Ohio

GINGERSNAPS

1 cup sugar
⅔ cup shortening
1 egg
4 tablespoons molasses
2 cups unbleached
   all-purpose flour
2 teaspoons baking soda
½ teaspoon each cloves,
   ginger, and cinnamon
½ teaspoon salt
Sugar

My mom used to make these when I was growing up. She got the recipe from my dad's mother, who would be well past 100 years old if she were alive today. These are still one of my dad's favorite cookies; and when he comes to our house and I have made them, there will be a lot fewer by the time he leaves. This year, I won a blue ribbon at the fair for these cookies. They can be made with either light or dark molasses, but I prefer the dark.

Cream together sugar, shortening, and egg. Add molasses and mix well. Sift together flour, soda, cloves, ginger, cinnamon, and salt, and stir into creamed mixture.

Roll dough into balls, then roll balls in sugar, and place on ungreased cookie sheets. Bake in preheated 350°F oven for 10 to 12 minutes, or until they start to color around the edges.

Yield: 3 dozen.

Sharon Evans
Rockwell, Iowa

CHRISTMAS THIMBLE COOKIES

❧

¾ cup (1½ sticks) butter, softened
½ cup brown sugar
1 egg yolk
½ teaspoon vanilla
¼ teaspoon salt
1½ cups unbleached all-purpose flour
2 egg whites
2 cups chopped nuts
⅓ cup raspberry jam

I grow my own raspberries and even make my own jam—just for these cookies. The recipe is my grandma's and is very old.

Cream together butter, sugar, egg yolk, and vanilla. Add salt and flour, and mix well. Chill dough for 1 hour.

Shape dough into balls about 1 inch in diameter. Dip each into unbeaten egg whites and roll in chopped nuts. Place on greased cookie sheets, and using a thimble or your thumb, make a depression in the top of each ball. Fill with jam. Bake in preheated 375°F oven until golden brown, about 15 minutes. Remove from oven and cool on racks.

Yield: 2 dozen.

Dawn Tenney
Wood Dale, Illinois

PERSIMMON COOKIES

❧

1 cup sugar
½ cup shortening
1 egg
1 cup persimmon pulp or applesauce
1 cup raisins
1 cup chopped nuts
2 cups unbleached all-purpose flour
1 teaspoon baking soda
1 teaspoon cinnamon
1 teaspoon vanilla or rum flavoring

Easy to make and even easier to eat, these are sweet, moist, and cakelike, and have an old-fashioned look.

Cream together sugar and shortening until light in consistency, then beat in egg. Add persimmon pulp, raisins, nuts, flour, soda, cinnamon, and vanilla. Stir until well blended.

Drop by spoonfuls onto ungreased cookie sheets and bake in preheated 350°F oven for 10 to 12 minutes.

Yield: 2 dozen.

Lea A. Scheid
Glen Ellyn, Illinois

APRICOT PASTRY HEARTS

&

1 cup unbleached
   all-purpose flour
⅛ teaspoon salt
½ cup (1 stick) margarine,
   cut into chunks
4 ounces cream cheese,
   cut into chunks
Apricot preserves
1 egg, beaten
Sugar

These tasty pastry hearts are attention-getters. A long time ago, I used to make them often. They are nice for ladies' luncheons, and children like them, too. The rich, flaky dough puffs up and browns beautifully (see page 49).

Measure flour and salt into bowl. Using a pastry blender or two knives, cut margarine and cream cheese into flour mixture until well blended. Gently shape dough into a ball and wrap in clear plastic. Refrigerate at least 2 hours or, preferably, overnight.

Preheat oven to 375°F. Lightly grease two cookie sheets. On floured surface, roll out dough ⅛-inch thick. With heart-shaped cookie cutter, cut out hearts. Reroll trimmings. Cut out once or twice again. On half the number of hearts, place 1 teaspoonful apricot preserves in center of each heart. Brush edges with beaten egg. Cover each with another cut-out heart. Lightly press edges together with a fork, sealing well. Arrange on cookie sheets, brush top of each with remainder of beaten egg, then sprinkle with sugar. Bake 10 to 12 minutes, or until golden. Cool on rack.

**Yield: 2 dozen hearts using a 3¼x2½-inch
   heart-shaped cutter.**

Susan M. Brown
Palmyra, Pennsylvania

KIFLE COOKIES

❧

1 cup (2 sticks) butter,
  softened
1 cup cottage cheese
  (small-curd)
2 cups unbleached
  all-purpose flour
¾ cup ground walnuts
¾ cup brown sugar
4 tablespoons butter, melted

An exquisite cookie—like a sweet-filled croissant but without all the work (see page 134). Easy to make and bake immediately, or freeze and bake as needed. Irresistible straight from the oven, but equally good a few days later— if any are left!

Beat 1 cup butter until smooth, then mix in cottage cheese. Add flour and blend thoroughly. (Dough should be slightly moist but not too wet.)

Divide dough into 6 equal balls and roll each out on lightly floured surface to 10-inch-diameter circle. Cut each circle into 8 wedges (as if slicing a pie).

Mix ground walnuts, brown sugar, and melted butter until completely blended. Place teaspoonful of filling onto base (wide end) of each wedge and roll up toward pointed end. Place on cookie sheets and bake in preheated 400°F oven for 20 minutes.

Yield: 4 dozen.

Milan Radan
Port Townsend, Washington

FAMILY TREASURE BUTTERHORNS

❧

DOUGH
4 cups unbleached
  all-purpose flour
1¼ cups (2½ sticks) butter
½ teaspoon salt
1 cake yeast
(continued)

This recipe is a true family treasure and—until now—a family secret. It has been passed down through at least three generations. While the fourth generation is too young to cook, the great-great-grandchildren look forward to this taste of family history at our traditional Christmas Day brunch. Busy as I may be preparing for a family celebration, the making of these butterhorns always energizes me and makes me most nostalgic, since they symbolize the continuity of a loving family.

In large bowl, combine flour, butter, salt, and yeast with pastry blender until mixture is crumbly. Make a well in center and add sour cream, vanilla, and egg yolks, and mix

½ cup sour cream
1 teaspoon vanilla
4 egg yolks

FILLING
4 egg whites
1 cup sugar
1 teaspoon vanilla
½ teaspoon almond extract
¼ pound pecans, ground
Confectioners' sugar

well. Divide dough into 6 portions and set aside.

Prepare filling next. Beat egg whites until almost stiff, add sugar, vanilla, and almond extract, and beat until stiff. Fold in pecans.

Sprinkle confectioners' sugar onto a surface and roll each of the 6 portions of dough into an 8- to 9-inch circle. Spread with filling, then cut each circle into 8 wedges. Starting from wide end, roll up each wedge. Place on ungreased cookie sheets and bake in preheated 325°F oven for 20 to 30 minutes, or until lightly browned.

Note: Although this recipe may appear time-consuming and complicated, it is easily done over a two-day period. The dough can be made one evening and refrigerated overnight in its six portions along with the reserved egg whites; all should be covered tightly. After bringing the dough and egg whites to room temperature the next evening, the butterhorns can be assembled and baked. Since they freeze well, they can be made ahead of time and enjoyed as needed—just thaw them at room temperature for several hours.

Yield: 4 dozen.

Susan G. Martin
Lake Barrington, Illinois

DATE-FILLED COOKIES

&

FILLING
2 cups (1 pound) whole dates,
    pitted and cut up
1 cup water
1 cup sugar

COOKIE DOUGH
1 cup sugar
1 cup (2 sticks) margarine,
    softened
1 egg
½ cup milk
1 teaspoon vanilla
1 teaspoon salt
1 teaspoon baking soda
2 cups oats
2 cups unbleached
    all-purpose flour

My great-grandma, Lydia Gaeth, first started baking these cookies in the 1930s in York, Nebraska. It is said that she always had a fresh batch waiting for visitors. Handed down for four generations, this recipe is still a family favorite (see page 130).

Make filling first. Combine dates, water, and sugar in saucepan and cook over low heat. Stir occasionally until dates cook into a paste. Remove from heat and set aside while making dough.

Cream together sugar and margarine. Beat in egg, milk, and vanilla. Add salt, soda, oats, and flour, and blend thoroughly.

Roll out half the dough on generously floured surface. Using a cookie or biscuit cutter or an inverted glass dipped in flour, cut out circles. Place on lightly greased or nonstick cookie sheets. Spoon a tablespoonful of date paste onto the center of each circle, but do not spread to the edges. Roll out remaining half of dough and cut out same number of circles. Place top circle over filling and seal to bottom circle by pressing around the edges with a fork. Bake in preheated 350°F oven for 15 minutes, or until light brown.

Yield: About 3 dozen, depending on size of cutter used.

Jennifer Sanders Wann
Murray, Kentucky

HAZELNUT MERINGUES

2 egg whites
1 cup sugar
1½ cups ground hazelnuts

Melt-in-your-mouth cookies that are simple yet distinctive. The most time-consuming part is preparing the hazelnuts. Place them on a cookie sheet in a 275°F oven for about 15 minutes, stirring occasionally. Remove from oven and rub them together to remove the skins.

Beat egg whites until foamy. Gradually add sugar while beating until whites become stiff but not dry. Fold in ground nuts. Drop by rounded teaspoonfuls, leaving 2 inches between each. Bake in preheated 300°F oven for 25 minutes, or until set and dry, but not brown.

Yield: 5 dozen.

Scott Ruhren
College Park, Maryland

JANHAGEL COOKIES

1 cup (2 sticks) butter or margarine, melted
1 cup sugar
1 egg, separated
2 cups unbleached all-purpose flour
1 teaspoon cinnamon
1 cup chopped pecans

This German cookie recipe came about when hard times forced cooks to be creative with standard ingredients. Simplicity at its best.

Combine butter and sugar, and blend well. Stir in egg yolk. Add flour and cinnamon, mixing thoroughly. Press mixture into greased, wax-paper-lined 10x15-inch jelly-roll pan. Beat egg white until fluffy, spread over cookie mixture, and sprinkle with pecans, pressing lightly into mixture.

Bake in preheated 350°F oven for 20 minutes, or until lightly browned. Let cool 5 minutes before cutting into 2x3-inch rectangles.

Yield: 2 dozen.

Freda Holmes
Oklahoma City, Oklahoma

CHRISTMAS CASSEROLE COOKIES

❧

2 eggs
1 cup sugar
1 teaspoon vanilla
¼ teaspoon almond extract
1 cup chopped walnuts or pecans
1 cup snipped dates
1 cup shredded coconut
Sugar for rolling

When my children were small, this was something they were able to "help" me bake for Christmas. Now that they are grown, they have passed this family tradition on to their own children.

Beat eggs well, then add sugar gradually while beating until fluffy. Stir in remaining ingredients and turn into ungreased 2-quart casserole. Bake in preheated 350°F oven for 30 minutes. Remove from oven and stir well with wooden spoon. Cool, form into small balls, and roll in additional sugar. Cool thoroughly.

Yield: 3 dozen.

Patricia S. Blair
East Peoria, Illinois

SHORTBREAD

❧

1½ cups unbleached
   all-purpose flour
¼ cup sugar
Dash of salt
1½ sticks butter, softened
Sugar for sprinkling

A true classic that belongs in everyone's repertoire of cookie recipes.

Mix flour, sugar, and salt in bowl. Work butter in with your fingers until soft dough is formed, then knead until soft and smooth, about 5 to 10 minutes. Press dough into greased 8-inch round pan. Smooth over top with knife. Mark top into 8 or 16 portions, then prick surface with fork.

Bake on middle shelf in preheated 350°F oven for 40 minutes. Remove from oven and cut all the way through the marked pieces. Leave in pan until almost completely cooled, then sprinkle with sugar and finish cooling on rack.

Yield: 8 to 16 wedges.

B. J. Strong
Anchorage, Alaska

LEMON BARS

∂

CRUST
2 cups unbleached
   all-purpose flour
½ cup confectioners' sugar
2 sticks butter or margarine

FILLING
4 eggs, beaten
6 tablespoons fresh lemon juice
   (about 4 lemons)
1 teaspoon grated lemon zest
2 cups granulated sugar
4 tablespoons unbleached
   all-purpose flour
1 teaspoon baking powder
Confectioners' sugar (optional)

My grandmother, Mommy, made these frequently for church events, bridge club, and visiting children and grandchildren. At age 96, she no longer cooks, so I was given her recipe file, which includes this as well as numerous other cards, written in her very familiar hand. When I make these, I enjoy not only their sweet-tart taste but also the special memories they evoke. These popular bars, with their shortbread crust and lemony filling, fit any occasion—and any mood.

For the crust, combine flour and confectioners' sugar in bowl. Cut in butter with pastry blender or two knives until mixture has a crumbly consistency. Press into 9x13-inch pan and bake in preheated 350°F oven for 20 minutes.

Meanwhile, prepare the filling. Combine eggs, lemon juice and zest, sugar, flour, and baking powder, beating until smooth. Pour over baked crust, return to oven, and bake 20 to 25 minutes. Remove from oven and let cool. Sprinkle with additional confectioners' sugar, if desired.

Yield: 3 dozen.

Sandra Taylor
Hancock, New Hampshire

HERMITS

ి

1½ cups dark brown sugar
⅔ cup shortening
4 tablespoons molasses
2 eggs, beaten
2½ cups unbleached
   all-purpose flour
½ teaspoon salt
1 teaspoon baking soda
1 teaspoon cinnamon
1 teaspoon nutmeg
1 teaspoon cloves
1 cup raisins
1 cup chopped walnuts
   (optional)

When in need of some "comfort food," make these dark-brown, spicy bars. They will fill your house with a wonderful aroma and your thoughts with happy memories. Take care not to overbake them.

Beat together brown sugar, shortening, and molasses until fluffy. Add eggs and mix well. Combine flour, salt, soda, and spices, and stir into wet ingredients, mixing thoroughly. Add raisins and nuts, if using.

With a greased spatula or greased fingertips, spread batter onto greased 10x13-inch cookie sheet. Bake in preheated 350°F oven for 15 to 18 minutes. Cool and cut into squares.

Yield: 2 dozen 2-inch squares.

Mary West
Osterville, Massachusetts

JAM BARS

ి

1 cup (2 sticks) margarine,
   softened
½ cup granulated sugar
½ cup brown sugar
2 cups unbleached
   all-purpose flour
1 teaspoon baking soda
½ cup oats
½ cup wheat germ
1 cup blackberry jam
   (or flavor of preference)

When I was a teenager in the 1950s, my friend Nancy and I would walk to her house after school. Often, her mom had just baked a pan of these bars, and she would invite me in to enjoy them. They were so good fresh out of the oven with a glass of milk. I still enjoy them to this day.

Cream margarine and sugars thoroughly. Add flour, soda, oats, and wheat germ, and mix well. Divide dough in half and pat one half into 9x13-inch pan. Spread jam over dough, then crumble remaining half of dough over jam, pressing down lightly. Bake in preheated 375°F oven for 30 minutes. Cool completely, then cut into bars.

Yield: 4 dozen.

Beverly A. Nyland
Wayland, Michigan

RASPBERRY BARS

ॐ

CRUST

1 cup unbleached
    all-purpose flour
½ cup (1 stick) butter or
    margarine, softened
¼ cup confectioners' sugar

FILLING

2 eggs, slightly beaten
1 cup granulated sugar
¼ cup unbleached
    all-purpose flour
½ teaspoon baking powder
¼ teaspoon salt
½ teaspoon cinnamon
1 teaspoon vanilla
1 tablespoon lemon juice
½ cup shredded coconut
1 cup fresh or frozen unsweetened
    raspberries (if frozen, thaw and
    drain well before measuring)
Confectioners' sugar (optional)

This recipe originally called for blueberries, but one year when we had an abundance of raspberries on hand, I used them instead. The bars were so appealing that my family has insisted ever since that I always use raspberries. (See page 133.)

For crust, mix flour, butter, and confectioners' sugar until smooth. Spread over bottom of lightly greased 8-inch square pan and bake in preheated 350°F oven for 25 minutes.

Prepare filling next. Beat together eggs, granulated sugar, flour, baking powder, salt, cinnamon, vanilla, and lemon juice. Stir in coconut and raspberries. Pour over top of hot, baked crust and bake 30 minutes more, or until top is golden. Cool before cutting into bars. If desired, dust lightly with additional confectioners' sugar.

Yield: 2 dozen.

Wendy Wellnitz
Eagan, Minnesota

91

YUMMY RHUBARB SQUARES

❧

CRUST
1 cup unbleached
   all-purpose flour
⅓ cup confectioners' sugar
6 tablespoons butter or margarine

FILLING
¼ cup unbleached
   all-purpose flour
1¼ cups granulated sugar
½ teaspoon salt
2 eggs, slightly beaten
3 cups diced fresh rhubarb

TOPPING
¾ cup unbleached
   all-purpose flour
½ cup granulated sugar
½ teaspoon cinnamon
⅓ cup butter or margarine

Perfect for summer entertaining, this pretty dessert has a buttery crust, sweetened rhubarb filling, and crumbly topping. For added splendor, serve with whipped cream or ice cream.

Make crust by combining flour and confectioners' sugar and then cutting in butter until mixture is crumbly. Press in bottom of greased 9-inch square pan. Bake in preheated 350°F oven for 12 to 13 minutes, or until lightly browned, and remove from oven. (It will not be completely baked.)

Mix filling ingredients in large bowl and pour over partially baked crust. Set aside.

For topping, combine flour, sugar, and cinnamon. Cut in butter until mixture has crumbly consistency, then sprinkle over filling. Bake another 45 minutes, or until topping is light golden brown and rhubarb is tender.

Yield: Nine 3-inch squares.

Fran Shaffer
West Caln, Pennsylvania

APRICOT BARS

৯৯

2½ cups unbleached
  all-purpose flour
2 tablespoons sugar
1 teaspoon salt (optional)
1 cup (2 sticks) margarine
1 cake yeast (or 1 package
  dry yeast)
½ cup warm water
1 teaspoon sugar
1 egg, beaten
1 teaspoon vanilla
1 jar (16 ounces) apricot jam
  or preserves
⅓ cup sugar

A versatile, fancy-looking dessert that requires very little effort. The crust is flaky, coated with a sugar glaze, and puffed slightly. Fill with other jams or preserves to vary the taste and color.

Combine flour, 2 tablespoons sugar, and salt, if using. Cut in margarine as for pie crust. Stir together yeast, warm water, and 1 teaspoon sugar, and set aside to soften. Beat together egg and vanilla. Add yeast mixture and blend well. Pour into flour mixture and stir.

Divide dough into 2 equal parts. Roll or pat one part on floured surface into a 10x13-inch rectangle ¼-inch thick. Transfer to lightly greased cookie sheet. Spread half the preserves lengthwise down the center, covering three-quarters width of the dough. Fold outer edges toward center so that they meet but do not overlap. (The folded bar should measure about 5x13 inches.)

Repeat with other half of dough and jam. Sprinkle ⅓ cup sugar evenly over both folded bars. Bake in preheated 375°F oven for 15 to 20 minutes, or until edges turn light brown. Let cool completely, then cut into 1½-inch-thick slices. (Cut in half again if smaller portions are desired.)

Yield: 26 to 52 bars.

Dorothy Payne
Ulysses, Nebraska

SINBAD BARS

૭

1 cup (2 sticks) butter
4 squares (1 ounce each)
  unsweetened chocolate
2½ cups sugar
4 eggs
1 cup unbleached
  all-purpose flour
½ teaspoon salt
2 teaspoons vanilla
1 package (8 ounces)
  cream cheese, softened

To turn these sinfully delicious bars into an elegant-looking dessert, melt ½ cup semi-sweet chocolate chips and 1½ teaspoons shortening together in a double boiler. Using a fine pastry tip, pipe lines across the top of warm or cooled bars that have been cut on the diagonal. (See page 133.)

In heavy-bottomed pot or double boiler, melt butter and unsweetened chocolate. In large bowl, beat 2 cups of the sugar and 3 of the eggs thoroughly. Stir in flour, salt, and 1 teaspoon vanilla. Slowly add chocolate mixture and blend completely.

In small bowl, beat cream cheese, remaining ½ cup sugar, remaining egg, and remaining teaspoon vanilla until smooth. Spread chocolate mixture on bottom of greased 9x13-inch pan and cover with cream-cheese mixture, spreading as best you can. Bake in preheated 350°F oven for 40 to 45 minutes.

Yield: 1½ dozen.

Sharon Haggerty
Washington, New Jersey

OH HENRY BARS

૭

BASE
4 cups quick-cooking oats
½ cup granulated sugar
1 cup packed brown sugar
2 sticks butter or
  margarine, melted
(continued)

These could become addictive for chocolate lovers and peanut butter cravers alike. They have a crunchy bottom and peanutty-chocolate top. Ideal for potluck suppers or bake sales.

To make base, combine oats and sugars in large bowl. Add melted butter and mix well. Press into greased 9x13-inch pan and bake in preheated 350°F oven for 15 to 20 minutes. Cool for 20 minutes.

Meanwhile, prepare topping. Melt together chocolate chips and peanut butter, stirring to blend. Spread on top of cooled

TOPPING
1 package (6 ounces) semi-sweet
  chocolate chips
1 cup crunchy peanut butter

cookie base and refrigerate for 1 hour. Cut into squares before serving.

Yield: 3 dozen.

Margaret Chernewski
Milford, New Hampshire

CHEWY GRANOLA BARS

❧

1 cup packed brown sugar
⅔ cup peanut butter
  (creamy or chunky)
½ cup corn syrup (light or dark)
½ cup butter, melted
2 teaspoons vanilla
3 cups oats (rolled or
  quick-cooking)
⅓ cup wheat germ
  (regular or honey-crunch)
2 tablespoons sesame seeds

OPTIONS (all, some, or none)
1 cup chips (chocolate, carob,
  peanut butter, or vanilla, or
  any combination)
½ cup raisins or dates
½ cup coconut
½ cup chopped nuts or
  sunflower seeds

These delicious and nutritious bars are special because they are always different! The options will satisfy anyone's preferences for favorite combinations.

In large bowl, combine brown sugar, peanut butter, corn syrup, butter, and vanilla, and blend well. Stir in oats, wheat germ, and sesame seeds. Fold in any options, if desired. Press mixture evenly into greased 9x13-inch pan and bake in preheated 350°F oven for 15 to 20 minutes, or until light brown. Cool completely before cutting into bars.

Yield: 2 dozen.

Mary Grace Clement
Avon Lake, Ohio

BLONDE BROWNIES

ð

2 cups unbleached
  all-purpose flour
1 teaspoon salt
1 teaspoon baking powder
¼ teaspoon baking soda
1 cup chopped walnuts or pecans
⅔ cup margarine, butter,
  or shortening
2 cups brown sugar
2 eggs, beaten
2 teaspoons vanilla
1 package (12 ounces)
  semi-sweet chocolate chips

This was one of my first projects as my mother's ''kitchen helper'' when I began to cook (and love it) about 15 years ago. These brownies are great fresh from the oven, but are even better if allowed to sit overnight.

In large bowl, sift together flour, salt, baking powder, and soda. Stir in nuts and set aside. Melt margarine and remove from heat. Stir in brown sugar and allow to cool.

Beat together eggs and vanilla, and blend into cooled margarine-and-sugar mixture. (Batter will be sticky and dense.) Add flour-and-nuts mixture, and stir until well blended. Spread in greased 9x13-inch pan and sprinkle chocolate chips evenly over top. Bake in preheated 350°F oven for 20 to 30 minutes, or until golden and edges pull away from sides of pan. Do not overbake.

Yield: 2 dozen.

Scott Ruhren
College Park, Maryland

BEST-EVER BROWNIES

ð

½ cup sifted unbleached
  all-purpose flour
⅓ to ½ cup cocoa
⅓ cup butter, melted
1 cup sugar
2 eggs
1 teaspoon vanilla
½ cup chopped nuts (optional)
1 cup semi-sweet chocolate
  chips (optional)

I've been making these quick and easy brownies for more than 20 years. I've tried other recipes, but nothing else compares.

Sift flour and cocoa together, and set aside. In medium-size bowl, combine cooled melted butter, sugar, eggs, and vanilla, mixing well. Stir in flour-and-cocoa mixture, and blend thoroughly. Add nuts and chocolate chips, if using, and mix well. Spread in greased 6x10-inch pan and bake in preheated 350°F oven for 25 minutes, or until brownies spring back when lightly touched.

Yield: 1 dozen.

Nancy Ritchey
Newport News, Virginia

TWEED SQUARES

ða

BASE

½ cup (1 stick) butter,
    softened
⅔ cup granulated sugar
1⅓ cups unbleached
    all-purpose flour
2 teaspoons baking powder
Few grains of salt
½ cup milk
2 squares (1 ounce each)
    unsweetened chocolate,
    grated (not too fine)
2 egg whites, beaten

FROSTING

⅓ cup butter, softened
1½ cups confectioners' sugar
2 egg yolks
1 teaspoon vanilla

CHOCOLATE GLAZE

2 squares (1 ounce each)
    unsweetened chocolate
2 tablespoons butter

I have no idea where this recipe originated, but the baked squares have a "tweedy" look and are very tasty, but not too sweet.

To make base, cream butter and granulated sugar in large bowl. Sift together flour, baking powder, and salt, then add alternately with milk to creamed mixture. Fold in grated chocolate, then beat in egg whites. Pour into greased 10-inch square pan and bake in preheated 350°F oven for 25 minutes.

Remove from oven and set aside to cool while preparing the frosting. Beat together butter and confectioners' sugar until smooth. Add egg yolks and vanilla, and beat well. Spread over cooled base.

For the glaze, melt chocolate with butter and drizzle over frosted squares.

Yield: 9 to 16 squares.

Jaine Parry
Apple Valley, Minnesota

MUFFINS

ALMOND & POPPY-SEED MUFFINS

❧

½ cup (1 stick) butter or
  margarine, softened
2 cups sugar
2 eggs
1 cup plain yogurt
2 teaspoons almond extract
2 cups unbleached
  all-purpose flour
3 teaspoons poppy seeds
½ teaspoon salt
¼ teaspoon baking soda
Sliced almonds

Very sweet and aromatic with a slight crunch from poppy seeds and almonds. These are almost like a dessert; if you want to boost their nutrition, reduce the total amount of sugar by half and use low-fat or nonfat plain yogurt.

In large bowl, cream together butter and 1 cup of the sugar. Beat in eggs, one at a time, then stir in yogurt and almond extract. In separate bowl, combine flour, poppy seeds, salt, remaining 1 cup sugar, and soda. Add to creamed mixture and blend just until moistened. Pour into greased muffin cups, filling three-quarters full. Sprinkle each muffin with sliced almonds and bake in preheated 400°F oven for 15 to 20 minutes.

Yield: 1 dozen.

Sandra Engelbrecht
Ilion, New York

JOAN PEARSON'S APPLE MUFFINS

❧

4 cups peeled, cored,
  and diced apples
2 cups sugar
2 eggs, beaten
⅔ cup oil
1 teaspoon vanilla
3 cups unbleached
  all-purpose flour
2 teaspoons baking soda
2 teaspoons baking powder
1 teaspoon salt
2 teaspoons cinnamon
½ cup raisins
½ cup chopped walnuts

Ideal for lunch boxes and after-school treats. The batter can also be baked in two 8-inch square pans for about 40 minutes and served as cake.

In large bowl, toss together apples and sugar, and let sit 10 minutes. Add eggs, oil, and vanilla, and mix well.

In another large bowl, combine flour, soda, baking powder, salt, and cinnamon. Add apple mixture and stir to blend. Fold in raisins and nuts. Spoon into 24 greased muffin cups and bake in preheated 350°F oven for 15 to 20 minutes.

Yield: 2 dozen.

Laurie DiCesare
Colchester, Vermont

APPLE SURPRISE MUFFINS

2 medium apples, peeled,
  cored, and diced
½ teaspoon cinnamon
1 tablespoon sugar
¼ cup chopped nuts
¼ cup (½ stick) butter or
  margarine, melted
¼ cup cocoa
¾ cup applesauce
1¼ cups unbleached
  all-purpose flour
½ cup sugar
¾ teaspoon baking soda
¼ teaspoon salt
1 egg, slightly beaten

Lovely chocolate muffins with bits of apples and nuts. Appealing to both children and adults.

Combine apples, cinnamon, 1 tablespoon sugar, and nuts in small bowl and set aside. Blend together melted butter and cocoa, and stir in applesauce. In medium-size bowl, combine flour, ½ cup sugar, soda, and salt. Stir in cocoa mixture and egg just until moistened.

Spoon 1 tablespoon batter into each of 12 greased or paper-lined muffin cups. Top with 1 heaping tablespoon of apples, pressing into batter, then cover each with another tablespoon of batter. Bake in preheated 375°F oven for 20 minutes.

Yield: 1 dozen.

Cyndi Hale
Northville, Michigan

OATS & APPLESAUCE MUFFINS

¾ cup unbleached
  all-purpose flour
½ teaspoon cinnamon
¼ teaspoon nutmeg
½ teaspoon salt
1 tablespoon baking powder
¾ cup cut-up dried prunes
1¼ cups rolled oats
½ cup brown sugar
½ cup oil
1 egg
1 cup unsweetened applesauce

My co-worker Darcy gave me this recipe, which I've nick-named Darcy Lune Prune Magoons. They taste like gourmet muffins and are a big hit with everyone who tries them.

Sift together flour, cinnamon, nutmeg, salt, and baking powder. In separate bowl, combine prunes, oats, and brown sugar, and add to flour mixture.

Beat together oil and egg, and stir in applesauce. Add to dry ingredients and mix lightly. Spoon into greased muffin cups and bake in preheated 400°F oven for 20 minutes.

Yield: 1 dozen.

Marg Meyers
Mt. Airy, Maryland

SPECIAL MUFFINS

෨

1¼ cups unbleached
    all-purpose flour
1 cup oat bran
2 teaspoons baking soda
1 teaspoon baking powder
½ teaspoon salt
2 teaspoons cinnamon
¾ cup brown sugar
1½ cups shredded carrots
2 large apples, peeled,
    cored, and shredded
½ cup raisins
1 cup chopped pecans
2 tablespoons oil
¼ cup applesauce
½ cup skim milk
2 eggs, beaten
1 teaspoon vanilla

These are so good they can be eaten hot or cold, with a meal or for breakfast, or just as a snack. They freeze beautifully, are a good source of fiber, and have very little fat. (To reduce the fat even more, bake in ungreased, paper-lined tins.)

Combine flour, oat bran, soda, baking powder, salt, and cinnamon in large bowl. Mix in brown sugar. Add carrots, apples, raisins, and nuts, and stir well. Make a well in center and add oil, applesauce, milk, eggs, and vanilla. Stir just until moistened.

Use ¼-cup measure to scoop batter into greased or paper-lined muffin cups. Bake in preheated 375°F oven for 20 minutes, or until nicely browned.

Yield: 1½ dozen.

Francine Derus
Westlake, Oregon

NORTH WOODS MUFFINS

෨

2 cups sifted unbleached
    all-purpose flour
½ cup sugar
1 tablespoon baking powder
½ teaspoon salt
4 tablespoons butter, melted
¾ cup milk or buttermilk
2 eggs
½ cup blueberries
½ cup cranberries
1 cup cooked wild rice

Golden muffins flecked with red, white, and blue. These are hearty, subtly sweet, and unusual. They make a fine accompaniment to just about any meal—a soup-and-salad lunch; Sunday brunch; or pork roast, chicken, or ham supper.

Combine flour, sugar, baking powder, and salt. In separate bowl, beat cooled melted butter, milk, and eggs. Pour into dry ingredients and stir until smooth. Fold in berries and rice. Fill greased muffin cups three-quarters full and bake in preheated 375°F oven for 20 minutes, or until done.

Yield: 1½ dozen.

Kay Englund
Ham Lake, Minnesota

BROWN-SUGAR OATMEAL MUFFINS

❧

1 cup rolled oats
1 cup whole-wheat flour
½ cup unbleached
   all-purpose flour
2 teaspoons baking powder
¼ teaspoon salt
½ to ¾ teaspoon allspice
   (or 1 teaspoon cinnamon, or
   ¼ teaspoon nutmeg or cloves)
2 large eggs
¾ cup packed dark brown sugar
¾ cup milk
¼ cup (½ stick) butter or
   margarine, melted (or oil)
1 teaspoon vanilla
½ cup raisins (or sunflower
   seeds, chopped walnuts,
   currants, or chopped dates)

These are a favorite of mine because I always have the ingredients on hand. Since I rarely have time to eat breakfast, I take these to work and briefly heat them in the microwave. Wonderful with fresh coffee!

In large bowl, thoroughly mix oats, flours, baking powder, salt, and spice of choice. Whisk eggs and brown sugar in another bowl, blending until smooth. Add milk, cooled melted butter, vanilla, and raisins to egg mixture, and blend well. Pour over dry ingredients and quickly fold in with rubber spatula, just until dry ingredients are moistened. Use ¼-cup measure to scoop batter into greased or paper-lined muffin cups. Bake in preheated 400°F oven for 20 to 25 minutes.

Yield: 1 dozen.

*Ingrid J. Apel
Ann Arbor, Michigan*

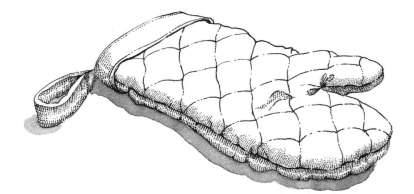

Banana Muffins

❧

2½ cups mashed bananas
2 eggs
1 cup sugar
¼ cup light molasses
1 cup canola oil
1 teaspoon cinnamon
1 teaspoon baking powder
2 teaspoons baking soda
3 cups whole-wheat flour
1 cup chopped walnuts
1 cup raisins

Soft, moist, and fragrant with bananas and cinnamon, these received our recipe tester's highest marks: "The best banana muffins I've ever tasted!"

Mix together bananas, eggs, sugar, molasses, and oil, beating well. In separate bowl, combine cinnamon, baking powder, soda, and flour. Make a well in center, pour in banana mixture, and stir lightly. Fold in nuts and raisins. Pour into greased or paper-lined muffin cups, filling three-quarters full, and bake in preheated 350°F oven for about 15 minutes. Cool completely and store in refrigerator.

Yield: 2 to 2½ dozen.

Susan Graber
Sedalia, California

Raspberry Honey Banana Muffins

❧

4 tablespoons margarine, softened
⅓ cup honey
2 eggs, beaten
1 teaspoon vanilla
2 teaspoons baking powder
¼ teaspoon salt
½ cup mashed bananas
2 cups unbleached all-purpose flour
½ cup milk
2 cups raspberries
1 tablespoon sugar
¼ teaspoon nutmeg

Not-too-sweet muffins with a subtle banana flavor intermingled with bursts of raspberries. Appealing any time of day—at breakfast, mid-afternoon, or late evening. *(See page 135.)*

Grease 12 regular-size muffin cups, including the area between the cups. In medium-size bowl, beat together margarine, honey, eggs, vanilla, baking powder, and salt. Add bananas and stir to blend. Fold in half the flour, then half the milk; repeat with remaining flour and milk. Fold in raspberries.

Scoop batter into muffin cups. Mix together sugar and nutmeg, and sprinkle on top of batter. Bake in preheated 375°F oven for 25 to 30 minutes, or until golden brown. Let muffins cool before removing from pan.

Yield: 1 dozen.

Lynette Herlan
Fall City, Washington

NEVER-FAIL BLUEBERRY MUFFINS

❧

2½ cups unbleached
   all-purpose flour
¾ cup sugar
2 teaspoons baking powder
1 teaspoon baking soda
½ teaspoon salt
½ cup (1 stick) butter or
   margarine
1 cup vanilla yogurt,
   at room temperature
2 eggs, slightly beaten
1 teaspoon vanilla
1½ cups fresh blueberries
   (or thawed and drained frozen)

A foolproof recipe with excellent flavor. In the middle of winter when I'm making these muffins, I'm reminded of pleasant summer days picking blueberries in Wisconsin or Upper Michigan.

In large bowl, mix flour, sugar, baking powder, soda, and salt. With pastry blender, cut in butter until mixture resembles fine crumbs.

In small bowl, stir yogurt until creamy. Blend in eggs and vanilla. Pour all at once into flour mixture and stir until just moistened. Gently fold in blueberries. Fill generously greased muffin cups two-thirds full and bake in preheated 400°F oven for 15 to 20 minutes, or until golden brown. Remove from pans immediately. Serve warm.

Yield: 1½ to 2 dozen.

Carol Rand
Marshfield, Wisconsin

THE VERY, VERY BEST BLUEBERRY MUFFINS

❧

2 cups fresh blueberries
2 cups unbleached
   all-purpose flour
4 teaspoons baking powder
1 teaspoon salt
1 cup sugar
⅓ cup lard (do not substitute)
1 egg
1 cup minus 2 tablespoons milk

The only time I ever buy lard is when I make these old-fashioned, absolutely outstanding blueberry muffins. They are without a doubt the very, very best I've ever had, and I'm convinced it's because of the lard. Even though I know I shouldn't use it, I assuage my guilt by fixing these muffins for special occasions only.

Rinse and sort through blueberries, toss lightly with a dusting of flour, and set aside.

In large bowl, sift together flour, baking powder, salt, and sugar. Add lard and, using a pastry blender, work it into dry ingredients until mixture has a crumbly consistency. Beat together egg and milk, and add to flour mixture, stirring lightly.

(continued)

Fold in blueberries until well distributed, then spoon into greased or paper-lined muffin cups. Bake in preheated 425°F oven for about 20 minutes.

Yield: 1 dozen.

Sheila Kirkpatrick
Peterborough, New Hampshire

BLUEBERRY BUTTERMILK MUFFINS

ð

½ cup (1 stick) unsalted butter, softened
2 eggs
1 cup plus 2 tablespoons sugar
3 cups unbleached all-purpose flour (reserve 3 tablespoons for berries)
1 teaspoon baking powder
2 teaspoons baking soda
½ teaspoon salt
2 cups frozen blueberries
1 teaspoon vanilla
1¼ cups buttermilk

Fresh blueberries can be stored in zip-lock bags at the peak of the season. Don't wash them before freezing, however, for they are coated with a natural preservative. When ready to use the frozen berries, rinse, sort, and dust them with flour before adding to the batter. If you desire a sweeter muffin, sprinkle the tops with a mixture of cinnamon and sugar before baking.

Cream together butter, eggs, and sugar. In separate bowl, combine flour, baking powder, soda, and salt. Toss blueberries with reserved flour and set aside. Mix vanilla and buttermilk, and add in thirds to creamed mixture, alternating with dry ingredients. Fold berries into batter.

Spoon into greased muffin cups and bake in preheated 400°F oven for 15 to 18 minutes. Cool on rack.

Yield: 1½ to 2 dozen.

Chris Eng
Castro Valley, California

105

CRANBERRY, WALNUT & ORANGE MUFFINS

ঞ

2 navel oranges
1 cup chopped walnuts
1 cup cranberries (fresh or
    frozen), chopped if desired
⅓ cup butter, melted
1 egg
2 cups unbleached
    all-purpose flour
1 tablespoon baking powder
½ teaspoon salt (optional)
⅔ cup sugar plus 1 teaspoon
    for topping

These golden muffins have slightly fissured tops glinting with sugar crystals, and a lively, sweet-tart flavor. They add a fancy touch to a family meal or dinner party.

Grate zest from oranges and measure 4 teaspoons into medium-size bowl. Add walnuts and cranberries, and stir to combine. Squeeze juice from oranges and measure ⅔ cup. Combine juice, cooled melted butter, and egg, whisking until blended. In large bowl, mix flour, baking powder, salt (if using), and ⅔ cup sugar. Add liquid mixture and stir until blended. (Do not use mixer.) Fold in cranberry-nut mixture.

Spoon batter into 12 greased or paper-lined muffin cups, and sprinkle tops with remaining 1 teaspoon sugar. Bake in preheated 400°F oven for 20 to 25 minutes.

Yield: 1 dozen.

Krista Diego
Dennis, Massachusetts

RASPBERRY STREUSEL MUFFINS

ঞ

1½ cups unbleached
    all-purpose flour
½ cup sugar
2 teaspoons baking powder
½ cup milk
½ cup (1 stick) butter, melted
1 egg, beaten
1 cup fresh or frozen whole
    unsweetened raspberries, divided

(continued)

Every May I cook for 200 children at Camp Highlands and make these muffins. Each child gets one muffin for breakfast, along with eggs and sausage. It's a lot of work, but worth all the effort when I hear the children saying, "M-m-m-m . . . muffins!"

In large bowl, combine flour, sugar, and baking powder. Beat together milk, cooled melted butter, and egg, and add to flour mixture, stirring just until moistened.

Spoon about 1 tablespoon batter into each greased or paper-lined cup of 12-muffin tin. Divide half the raspberries among the cups, top with remaining batter, then add remaining raspberries.

(continued)

STREUSEL TOPPING
¼ cup chopped pecans
¼ cup packed brown sugar
¼ cup unbleached
  all-purpose flour
2 tablespoons butter, melted

For topping, combine pecans, brown sugar, flour, and butter. Sprinkle over batter and bake in preheated 350°F oven for 20 to 25 minutes, or until toothpick inserted in middle comes out clean.

Yield: 1 dozen.

Mary Detweiler
West Farmington, Ohio

MAGGIE'S RASPBERRY MUFFINS

ε&

1 cup fresh raspberries
  (or frozen if not in season)
1 to 3 tablespoons
  confectioners' sugar
½ cup (1 stick) butter, softened
1 cup granulated sugar
¼ cup sour cream
1 large egg
3 teaspoons grated lemon zest
1 teaspoon vanilla
1½ cups self-rising flour
½ cup oats
½ teaspoon baking soda
1 teaspoon cinnamon

Sweet yet tangy, with lots of flavor from the raspberries. To turn these into a breakfast muffin, you may want to reduce the granulated sugar to ½ cup and substitute plain yogurt for the sour cream.

Rinse fresh raspberries and pat dry; toss in confectioners' sugar until well coated and set aside. (If using frozen berries, drain well first.)

Combine butter, sugar, sour cream, egg, and lemon zest in large bowl. Stir in vanilla. In separate bowl, mix together flour, oats, soda, and cinnamon. Slowly add dry ingredients to butter mixture, blending until just moistened. Fold in raspberries.

Spoon batter into greased muffin cups, filling about two-thirds full. Bake in preheated 350°F oven for 18 to 22 minutes, or until they test done. Remove from cups and serve.

Yield: 1 dozen.

Fran Shaffer
West Caln, Pennsylvania

BLACK RASPBERRY MUFFINS

❧

1 cup unbleached
   all-purpose flour
⅔ cup whole-wheat flour
⅓ cup oat bran
4 teaspoons baking powder
1 teaspoon salt
¼ cup shortening
½ cup sugar
2 eggs, beaten
⅔ cup milk
⅓ cup chopped pecans
1½ cups fresh or frozen
   black raspberries (if frozen,
   thaw and drain well
   before measuring)

These are light yet hearty, and not too sweet. Just right for breakfast or brunch.

In medium-size bowl, combine flours, oat bran, baking powder, and salt. Mix well and set aside.

In large bowl, cream shortening, then gradually add sugar, beating well. Stir in eggs. Add dry mixture to creamed mixture alternately with milk, stirring until just moistened. Gently fold in pecans and black raspberries.

Fill greased muffin cups one-half to two-thirds full. Bake in preheated 400°F oven for about 20 minutes.

Yield: 1 to 1½ dozen.

Wendy Wellnitz
Eagan, Minnesota

UPSIDE-DOWN MUFFINS

❧

¼ cup (½ stick) butter or
   margarine, softened
2 tablespoons granulated sugar
1 egg
1 cup unbleached
   all-purpose flour
1½ teaspoons baking powder
¼ teaspoon salt
⅓ cup milk
(continued)

Gooey and delicious, these look like sticky buns. Great for a special-occasion brunch or holiday.

In large bowl, cream ¼ cup butter, sugar, and egg, beating until smooth and fluffy. Combine flour, baking powder, and salt, and add to creamed mixture alternately with milk, mixing well after each addition.

Spoon 1½ teaspoons melted margarine and 1 tablespoon pecans into each of 8 well-greased muffin cups. Combine brown sugar and cinnamon, mixing thoroughly, and divide mixture equally among the cups. Spoon in batter, filling cups two-thirds full.

¼ cup (½ stick) margarine, melted
½ cup chopped pecans
3 tablespoons brown sugar
¼ teaspoon cinnamon

Bake in preheated 400°F oven for 15 to 20 minutes. Remove from muffin cups immediately and spoon any sugar mixture that remains in cups over the warm muffins.

Yield: 8 muffins.

Mary Jane Christian
Lewisburg, West Virginia

Rhubarb Muffins

ह

2½ cups unbleached
    all-purpose flour
1¼ cups brown sugar
1 teaspoon baking powder
1 teaspoon baking soda
½ teaspoon salt
1 cup buttermilk
½ cup oil
1 egg
1⅓ cups diced rhubarb
    (well drained if frozen)
½ cup chopped walnuts
1 tablespoon butter, melted
⅓ cup granulated sugar
1 teaspoon cinnamon

This muffin combines the tang of spring rhubarb, the sweetness of brown sugar, and the slight crunch of a spicy topping, making any meal a feast. I like to think that pioneer ladies used their rhubarb this way.

In large bowl, sift together flour, brown sugar, baking powder, soda, and salt. In separate bowl, beat buttermilk, oil, and egg until well blended. Pour into dry ingredients and mix just until moistened.

Fold in rhubarb and nuts, and spoon mixture into greased muffin cups. Combine melted butter, granulated sugar, and cinnamon, and sprinkle on top of batter. Bake in preheated 425°F oven for 20 to 25 minutes. Remove from cups immediately.

Yield: 1 dozen.

Mary Yost
Barlow, Ohio

ORANGE-CHOCOLATE MUFFINS

ঌ

2 cups flour (unbleached
 all-purpose or
 whole-wheat pastry)
½ cup sugar
2 teaspoons baking powder
½ teaspoon baking soda
½ teaspoon salt
Grated zest of 1 orange
1 egg
⅓ cup oil
1 cup buttermilk or sour milk
1 cup semi-sweet chocolate chips

Great-tasting, perfect-looking muffins that are almost as light as cupcakes (see page 135). Popular with every age-group.

In large bowl, mix flour, sugar, baking powder, soda, salt, and orange zest. In separate bowl, beat together egg, oil, and buttermilk. Stir in chocolate chips, then add to dry ingredients, mixing just until moistened. Spoon into 12 large or 18 medium-size paper-lined muffin cups. Bake in preheated 400°F oven for 20 minutes.

Yield: 1 to 1½ dozen.

Susan Holec
Evansville, Wisconsin

BLACK-BOTTOM CUPS

ঌ

BASE
1½ cups sifted unbleached
 all-purpose flour
1 cup sugar
¼ cup cocoa
1 teaspoon baking soda
1 cup water
⅓ cup oil
1 tablespoon vinegar
1 teaspoon vanilla
(continued)

"Absolutely sinful!" reported our recipe tester. More like cupcakes than muffins, these are easy to make yet fancy-looking. Ideal for the holidays, as a special after-school snack, or for a child's birthday party.

For the base, sift flour, sugar, cocoa, and soda together into mixing bowl. Add water, oil, vinegar, and vanilla, and beat until well blended. Spoon into paper-lined muffin cups, filling one-third full.

For the topping, beat together cream cheese, egg, and sugar until smooth and fluffy. Stir in chocolate chips and mix until evenly incorporated.

(continued)

TOPPING

1 package (8 ounces)
    cream cheese, softened
1 egg
⅓ cup sugar
1 cup semi-sweet chocolate chips

Place a heaping tablespoonful of this mixture on top of batter in each muffin cup. Bake in preheated 350°F oven for about 30 minutes.

Yield: 1½ dozen.

Sandy Placek
Santa Rosa, California

LILLIE'S GINGERBREAD MUFFINS

❧

1 cup shortening
1 cup sugar
4 eggs
1 cup molasses
1 cup buttermilk
2 teaspoons baking soda
4 cups unbleached
    all-purpose flour
1 teaspoon salt
1 teaspoon cinnamon
½ teaspoon cloves
½ teaspoon allspice
2 teaspoons ginger
1 cup chopped dates, nuts,
    or raisins

Hot from the oven, these finely textured muffins are light and airy and literally melt in your mouth. An excellent balance of spices and subtle sweetness makes them appropriate for breakfast, lunch, or supper. They could even be frosted and served as dessert. The batter will keep in the refrigerator for up to six weeks if well covered, allowing you to make as many or as few as you want. Or do all the baking at one time, store them in the freezer, and remove as needed.

In large bowl, cream together shortening and sugar. Beat in eggs, one at a time, until light and fluffy. Stir in molasses.

Combine buttermilk and soda in small bowl. Sift together flour, salt, cinnamon, cloves, allspice, and ginger, and stir into creamed mixture alternately with buttermilk, blending thoroughly after each addition. Fold in dates, nuts, or raisins.

Spoon batter into greased or paper-lined muffin cups, filling two-thirds full, and bake in preheated 375°F oven for 20 to 25 minutes.

Yield: 4 to 5 dozen.

Dolly Pearson
Colorado Springs, Colorado

GOOD MUFFINS

&

2 cups unbleached
   all-purpose flour
1 cup granulated sugar
   (or less to taste)
¼ cup brown sugar
2 teaspoons baking powder
1 teaspoon baking soda
½ teaspoon salt
1 cup raisins
¾ cup chopped nuts
2 eggs
1 cup sour cream
6 teaspoons oil
1 teaspoon vanilla

These are rich, sweet, and nutty. Serve with afternoon tea, as an after-school snack, or as a light dessert. The recipe is adaptable to additions or variations of ingredients, so you can make these muffins from what you have on hand and to fit any need or occasion.

Mix together flour, sugars, baking powder, soda, and salt. Stir in raisins and nuts. Whisk together eggs, sour cream, oil, and vanilla. Make well in dry ingredients, pour in liquid mixture, and stir to combine. Spoon into 12 greased large muffin cups and bake in preheated 400°F oven for 20 to 25 minutes, or until they test done.

Yield: 1 dozen large.

Gladys Moran
Shohola, Pennsylvania

BOSTON BROWN-BREAD MUFFINS

&

½ cup rye flour
½ cup whole-wheat flour
½ cup yellow cornmeal or
   masa harina
¾ teaspoon salt
1½ teaspoons baking soda
1 egg
⅓ cup molasses
⅓ cup firmly packed brown sugar
⅓ cup oil
1 cup buttermilk
1 cup golden raisins

The combination of rye and whole-wheat flours plus cornmeal creates an unusual and appealing taste and texture that are further enhanced by golden raisins. These nutritious and delicious muffins will be made again and again.

In large bowl, and using a fork, mix together flours, cornmeal, salt, and soda. In small bowl, combine egg, molasses, brown sugar, oil, and buttermilk, beating until well blended. Pour egg mixture into flour mixture and stir just until moistened. Fold in raisins. Fill greased muffin cups about three-quarters full. Bake in preheated 400°F oven for 15 minutes, or until toothpick inserted into center comes out clean. Don't overbake. Serve hot.

Yield: 1 dozen.

Francine Derus
Westlake, Oregon

BRENDA'S BRAN MUFFINS

2½ cups Raisin Bran cereal
½ cup All-Bran cereal
¼ cup wheat germ
1¼ cups milk
1 egg
⅓ cup oil
1¼ cups self-rising flour
¼ cup sugar

I obtained this recipe years ago and have altered it each time I've made it. This is my favorite version, which I fix for breakfast or to serve with other meals. Healthful and delectable, these muffins are moist yet do not have an oily taste.

Mix cereals, wheat germ, and milk in large bowl, and let sit 1 to 2 minutes. Add egg and oil, and beat well. Blend together flour and sugar, then add to cereal mixture, stirring only until combined. Do not overmix. Spoon batter into 12 greased 2½-inch muffin cups and bake in preheated 400°F oven for 25 minutes.

Yield: 1 dozen.

Brenda G. Roberts
Smiths Grove, Kentucky

WINTER-SQUASH MUFFINS

1⅓ cups whole-wheat flour
2 teaspoons baking soda
½ teaspoon cinnamon
½ teaspoon nutmeg
¼ cup honey
1 cup winter squash or
  pumpkin puree
½ cup raisins
½ cup chopped walnuts
  or pecans
4 tablespoons butter or
  margarine, melted
1 egg, lightly beaten
½ cup buttermilk

The aroma and flavor of these muffins are most often associated with Thanksgiving, but they are appealing any time of the year. Our recipe tester said she has replaced her favorite pumpkin muffin recipe with this one because it not only tastes better but also uses a more healthful combination of ingredients.

In large bowl, sift together flour, soda, cinnamon, and nutmeg. Stir in honey, winter squash, raisins, nuts, and melted butter, blending well.

Add egg to the buttermilk and beat lightly, then blend into squash mixture. Spoon into greased muffin cups, filling two-thirds full, and bake in preheated 350°F oven for 18 to 20 minutes.

Yield: 1 dozen.

George Rector
Cullowhee, North Carolina

SWEET-POTATO MUFFINS

❧

½ cup (1 stick) butter or
   margarine, softened
½ cup granulated sugar
½ cup brown sugar
2 eggs
1¼ cups cooked, mashed
   sweet potatoes
¼ cup molasses
2 tablespoons milk
1½ cups unbleached
   all-purpose flour
2 teaspoons baking powder
¼ teaspoon salt (optional)
1 teaspoon cinnamon
¼ teaspoon nutmeg
¼ teaspoon allspice
½ cup raisins
¼ cup chopped pecans
   (optional)

I developed this years ago when I was trying to use up some sweet potatoes and found a recipe that called for them. After adding spices and other goodies, I ended up with this. These muffins are so light and fluffy, unlike any other I've tried. The recipe makes enough to freeze for later use.

In large bowl, cream butter and sugars until light and smooth. Add eggs, one at a time, beating thoroughly after each addition. Stir in sweet potatoes, molasses, and milk, blending well. Sift together flour, baking powder, salt (if using), and spices, and add to sweet-potato mixture, stirring until just moistened. Fold in raisins and nuts, if using.

Grease bottoms only of muffin cups. Spoon batter into cups, filling three-quarters full, and bake in preheated 400°F oven for 20 to 25 minutes.

Yield: 1½ dozen.

Nancy Ritchey
Newport News, Virginia

SMOKED-TURKEY MUFFINS

❧

½ cup chopped scallions
  (about 5)
1 teaspoon minced garlic
  (about 2 medium-size cloves)
2 tablespoons oil
½ cup chopped mushrooms
  (about 5 medium-size)
1 cup orange juice
1 egg, beaten
¾ cup diced smoked turkey
  (about 4 ounces)
1½ cups unbleached
  all-purpose flour
½ cup quick-cooking oats
2 teaspoons baking powder
¼ teaspoon salt
½ cup grated Swiss cheese
  (about 2 ounces)

This recipe was inspired by a muffin I had at a restaurant in northern Michigan. Actually a "mini meal in a muffin," they are perfect for lunch with a salad, for a picnic, or as an addition to a buffet table. They are easy to make and wholesome.

Saute scallions and garlic in oil for 2 minutes. Add mushrooms and cook for 1½ minutes. Cool, but do not drain.

Beat orange juice with egg, add mushroom mixture and turkey, and stir to blend. In large bowl, mix together flour, oats, baking powder, salt, and cheese. Pour in orange-juice mixture and stir just until moistened.

Line muffin cups with paper liners or use nonstick vegetable spray. Spoon mixture into cups and bake in preheated 425°F oven for 20 to 25 minutes.

Yield: 1 dozen.

*Linda Bankauskas
Ypsilanti, Michigan*

BISCUITS, BUNS & ROLLS

My Favorite Biscuits

❧

2 cups unbleached
    all-purpose flour
3 teaspoons baking powder
1 teaspoon salt
⅓ cup oil
⅔ cup milk
Butter

Light, flaky, good-looking biscuits to serve with breakfast, soup, or a casserole. Because they are made with oil, they are quicker, easier to toss together, and, if you use a good oil, healthier.

In bowl, mix flour, baking powder, and salt. Add oil and milk, and stir until well blended.

Turn out onto floured surface and knead about 10 times for smooth ball. Roll out and cut with biscuit cutter, or drop by large tablespoonfuls onto greased baking sheet. Bake in preheated 425°F oven for about 15 minutes, or until golden brown. Brush with butter while hot.

VARIATION
This recipe is versatile and can be used in other ways, too. Roll out dough; spread with mincemeat, or jelly and peanut butter, or apple butter; roll up like a jelly roll; and cut into 1-inch pieces. Then bake on a cookie sheet or in muffin cups.

Yield: 1 to 1½ dozen.

Mary Detweiler
West Farmington, Ohio

ANGEL FLAKE BISCUITS

≈

5 cups unbleached
   all-purpose flour
2 teaspoons baking powder
1 teaspoon baking soda
3 tablespoons sugar
1 teaspoon salt
¾ cup shortening
1 package dry yeast
¼ cup warm water
2 cups buttermilk

These are light and fluffy, and slightly sweet. I've had the recipe for many years and use it often.

Sift together flour, baking powder, soda, sugar, and salt. Mix well. Cut in shortening and blend until mixture is crumbly. Dissolve yeast in warm water, then add yeast mixture and buttermilk to dry ingredients and stir. Shape dough into ball, place in greased plastic bag, and seal tightly. Refrigerate for 12 hours.

Roll out dough on floured surface to ⅜-inch thickness, then cut as desired. Place on ungreased baking sheet and bake in preheated 450°F oven for about 10 minutes.

Yield: 3½ dozen 2-inch biscuits.

Carolyn Albright
Cairo, Missouri

BAKING POWDER BISCUITS

≈

2 cups sifted unbleached
   all-purpose flour
4 teaspoons baking powder
½ teaspoon salt
2 tablespoons sugar (optional)
½ teaspoon cream of tartar
½ cup shortening
⅔ cup milk
1 egg, unbeaten

These rise high and have a light, fluffy texture. Made with sugar, they are perfect for strawberry shortcake; without sugar, a fine addition to lunch or supper.

Sift flour, baking powder, salt, sugar (if using), and cream of tartar into bowl. Add shortening and cut in with pastry blender or two knives to a cornmeal-like consistency. Slowly stir in milk, add egg, and blend to combine.

Turn out onto floured surface and knead 5 times. Roll to ½-inch thickness and cut with cutter. Place on greased baking sheet and bake in preheated 450°F oven for 10 to 15 minutes, or until golden in color.

Yield: 1 dozen.

Sharon Evans   Kim Cox
Rockwell, Iowa   and   Lakin, Kansas

MASTER MIX FOR SOUTHERN BISCUITS

❧

MASTER MIX
4½ cups unbleached
   all-purpose flour
5 teaspoons baking powder
1 teaspoon salt
5 tablespoons shortening
3 tablespoons unsalted butter

SOUTHERN BISCUITS
1 cup Master Mix
⅓ cup milk or buttermilk

This recipe is for a biscuit mix that can be made in quantity and refrigerated in an airtight container for up to 3 months. Southern Biscuits, which are made from the mix, have repeatedly won blue ribbons at the Kentucky State Fair.

To make Master Mix, combine flour, baking powder, and salt in large bowl. Cut in shortening and butter with pastry blender or two knives until mixture resembles coarse meal. This makes 6 cups. Store in refrigerator and use as needed.

To make biscuits, combine Master Mix and milk on floured surface to make a soft dough. Do not overmix! Roll or press out to ½- to ¾-inch thickness. Cut with 2-inch round cutter and place on ungreased baking sheet. Bake in preheated 400°F oven for 20 minutes, or until golden brown on top.

Yield: ½ dozen.

J. William Klapper
Louisville, Kentucky

EASY BUTTERMILK BISCUITS

❧

4 cups unbleached
   all-purpose flour
6 to 10 tablespoons sugar
2 tablespoons baking powder
½ teaspoon baking soda
1 teaspoon salt
⅔ cup shortening
1½ cups buttermilk
   (or 1½ cups milk plus
   2 tablespoons white vinegar)

These biscuits are mouth-watering and very easy to make. They are faintly sweet, tender, and flaky with good loft.

In large bowl, combine flour, sugar, and baking powder. Stir in soda and salt. Cut in shortening and blend until mixture is crumbly. Add buttermilk, stirring lightly. (The dough will be a bit sticky, so add flour as needed.) Turn out onto floured surface and knead lightly. Roll or pat dough to about 1-inch thickness, cut with floured water glass or biscuit cutter, and place in buttered, shallow baking dish. Bake in preheated 400°F oven for 15 minutes.

Yield: 1½ dozen.

Sharon Frazier
Sagle, Idaho

MRS. L's BUTTERMILK BISCUITS

&

2 cups unbleached
   all-purpose flour
3 teaspoons baking powder
¼ teaspoon baking soda
½ teaspoon salt
5 rounded tablespoons shortening
1 scant cup buttermilk

These are the best baking powder biscuits I have ever eaten, and the key ingredient is buttermilk. They are high, light, moist, and absolutely scrumptious hot or not (see page 52). In addition to dinner biscuits, they also make excellent short-cakes to eat with fresh strawberries and cream. They can be stored for a day or two in a non-airtight container (leave the lid slightly ajar). To keep them longer, freeze or refrigerate.

Sift together flour, baking powder, soda, and salt. Cut in shortening with pastry blender until consistency is mealy. Add buttermilk and stir until well blended.

Turn onto floured surface, knead 18 times, and pat out to ¾-inch thickness. Cut biscuits with biscuit or cookie cutter and place on lightly greased baking sheet.

Bake in preheated 450°F oven for 12 minutes.

Yield: 1 to 2 dozen.

*Lea A. Scheid
Glen Ellyn, Illinois*

RICH SHORTCAKE BISCUITS

&

2 cups sifted unbleached
   all-purpose flour
1 teaspoon baking powder
1 teaspoon salt
½ teaspoon cream of tartar
1 tablespoon sugar
(continued)

The superior taste and texture of these biscuits makes them ideal for fresh strawberries and whipped cream, but they are equally compelling served for breakfast with butter and strawberry jam.

Sift flour, baking powder, salt, cream of tartar, and sugar into mixing bowl. Add shortening and cut in finely with pastry blender or two knives. Beat milk and egg together with a fork and add to dry ingredients, stirring until just blended. (Dough should be soft and puffy.)

Turn dough out onto floured surface and knead gently. Roll out to ½-inch thickness and cut with rim of glass or

½ cup shortening or margarine
¾ cup milk
1 egg

biscuit cutter. Place on ungreased baking sheet and bake in preheated 450°F oven for 12 to 15 minutes, or until golden in color.

Yield: 1 dozen.

Margaret Chernewski
Milford, New Hampshire

CREAMED-CORN BISCUITS

ஊ

2½ cups unbleached
   all-purpose flour
2 teaspoons baking powder
1½ teaspoons crushed dried
   hot red chilies
¼ teaspoon nutmeg
½ cup (1 stick) butter,
   cut in chunks
2 large eggs
1 small can (8¾ ounces)
   creamed corn
¼ cup sugar

These are truly delicious and different. Excellent with chili, soup, or stew. If you can't find hot red chilies, you might substitute dried red-pepper flakes.

In large bowl, mix flour, baking powder, chilies, and nutmeg. Rub in butter until mixture has consistency of coarse crumbs. In separate bowl, beat eggs, add creamed corn and sugar, and blend. Add to flour mixture and stir until just evenly moistened.

Scrape dough onto floured board, knead 6 to 8 times, and pat out to ½- to ¾-inch thickness. Cut rounds from dough with 2½-inch-diameter cutter. Place biscuits, slightly apart, on ungreased baking sheet, and bake in 400°F oven for 20 to 25 minutes, or until golden.

Yield: 15 biscuits.

Constance M. Ellway
Hailey, Idaho

GRANDMA'S FLUFFY BUNS

❧

1 package dry yeast
½ cup warm water
1 cup mashed potatoes
  (use a little potato water
  when mashing)
¾ cup canola or corn oil
½ cup sugar
1 teaspoon salt
2 eggs, beaten
1 cup milk, scalded and
  cooled to lukewarm
1 cup whole-wheat
  (or graham) flour
7 cups unbleached all-purpose
  flour (approximately)
1 egg white
Sesame seeds for topping

I have been a bread baker for 30 years, and this is my most-requested recipe. It came about when my daughter-in-law raved about the white "fluffy buns" served at a well-known restaurant chain here in Ohio. I decided to try to duplicate the buns but wanted them to be more nutritious and flavorful. The potatoes make them light, and the whole-wheat flour adds texture and color. The ball-in-circle design gives height and visual appeal.

Dissolve yeast in warm water and set aside. Cream together mashed potatoes, oil, sugar, salt, and eggs. Add cooled, scalded milk and yeast to potato mixture and blend well. Work in whole-wheat flour, then gradually add all-purpose flour until dough is stiff enough to handle.

Turn out onto floured surface and knead well. Place in large oiled bowl and turn once so that top is oiled. Cover and let rise until doubled in bulk.

Punch down and let rest for a few minutes, then roll out like biscuit dough to about ⅜- to ½-inch thickness. Cut out about 30 circles using a biscuit cutter. (You will have a considerable amount of leftover dough, which you will use to form the centers of the rolls.) Place circles in large, slightly greased baking pan or use several smaller pans.

With remaining dough, form 30 balls about 1½ inches in diameter. Push down with thumb in center of each circle and make a deep depression. Place a ball inside each depression in each circle. (You may have some dough left over, as it is difficult to estimate the exact number of rolls the dough will make. Just use whatever is left to make additional circles and balls.)

(continued)

Mix egg white with small amount of water and whisk until frothy. Brush tops of rolls using entire egg-white mix. This helps to hold the roll together, and it gives the crust a nice golden brown color. Sprinkle sesame seeds on top. Let rise, then bake in preheated 375°F oven for about 18 minutes, or until light brown.

Yield: About 2½ dozen.

Margaret Frizzell
Springboro, Ohio

JIFFY HAMBURGER BUNS

2&

4½ to 5 cups unbleached
   all-purpose flour
2 packages dry yeast
1 cup milk
¾ cup water
½ cup oil
¼ cup sugar
1 tablespoon salt

Quick, easy, and tasty, these could also work as dinner rolls. For those individuals watching their salt consumption, reduce the amount called for to 1½ teaspoons, or to taste.

Mix together 2 cups of the flour and the yeast. In small saucepan, combine milk, water, oil, sugar, and salt, and heat to 120°F. Add to flour mixture and beat until smooth. Keep adding more flour to make a soft dough, then let dough rest for 10 minutes.

Roll out on floured surface to about ½-inch thickness. Cut into rounds with 3-inch cutter and place on greased baking sheets. Let rise until doubled in bulk (about 25 minutes). Bake in preheated 425°F oven for about 15 minutes, or until golden brown.

Yield: 12 to 15 buns.

M. Thomson
Vellore, Madras, India

EASY SESAME BREADSTICKS OR BUNS

❧

2 cups milk
¼ cup canola oil
¼ cup honey
2 tablespoons (2 packages) dry yeast
1 teaspoon sugar
¼ cup warm water
6 cups unbleached all-purpose flour (approximately)
1 teaspoon salt
1 egg white
2 to 4 teaspoons sesame seeds

Whether made into breadsticks (see page 54) or buns, these are guaranteed to please every member of the family.

Scald milk, then mix with oil and honey. Set aside to cool.

In separate bowl, mix yeast, sugar, and water. Let sit a few minutes, then combine with milk mixture. Add 2 cups flour and beat until smooth. Let rest 10 minutes.

Mix salt with remaining 4 cups flour and gradually beat into milk-and-flour mixture until kneadable. Turn out onto floured surface and knead until smooth and elastic, adding flour as needed.

If making breadsticks, cut dough into 20 pieces, and with your palms, roll each piece into a rope about the length of a baking sheet. Place on oiled sheet and let rise 30 minutes.

If buns are desired, pinch off small handfuls of dough, shape into rolls, flatten slightly, and place on oiled baking sheet. Let rise 30 minutes.

Beat egg white, brush on tops of ropes or rolls, and sprinkle with sesame seeds. Bake in preheated 375°F oven for 20 minutes.

Yield: 20 sticks or 1 dozen buns.

Julie Ray
Decaturville, Tennessee

BISCUITS, BUNS & ROLLS

CINNAMON BUNS

❧

1 package dry yeast
¼ cup warm water
1 cup sour cream
3 tablespoons granulated sugar
⅛ teaspoon baking soda
1 teaspoon salt
1 egg
2 tablespoons margarine, softened
3 cups unbleached
   all-purpose flour
2 tablespoons butter, melted
⅔ cup dark brown sugar
2 teaspoons cinnamon
Confectioners' sugar

PECAN STICKY BUNS
Dough for Cinnamon Buns
⅓ cup butter
⅔ cup dark brown sugar
⅓ cup light corn syrup
⅓ cup coarsely broken pecans

Classic cinnamon rolls that require no kneading and no initial rising. I received the dough recipe from a friend and adapted it to make Cinnamon Buns and a variation I've also included called Pecan Sticky Buns.

Add yeast to warm water and set aside for 5 minutes. Stir in sour cream, granulated sugar, soda, salt, egg, margarine, and flour until well blended.

Turn dough onto lightly floured surface and knead a few times to completely mix dough. Cover with towel and let rest 10 minutes.

Roll dough into 12x20-inch rectangle and brush with melted butter. Combine brown sugar and cinnamon, and sprinkle over dough to within 1 inch of edges of rectangle. Starting on long side, roll up dough like a jelly roll and pinch seam to seal. Cut in crosswise slices, 1 inch wide, to make 18 pieces. Place pieces cut side down in 2 well-greased 8-inch round or square pans. Cover and let rise in warm place for 45 minutes to 1 hour, until doubled in bulk. Bake in preheated 375°F oven for 15 minutes. Turn out immediately on racks to cool. Frost while warm with confectioners' sugar mixed with enough water to form icing.

To make sticky buns, proceed as described above up to the point of placing dough in pans. Grease two 8-inch square pans (these have higher sides than round ones, which keeps the syrup from bubbling over during baking). In saucepan, bring butter, brown sugar, and corn syrup to a boil. Pour into bottom of pans and sprinkle each with pecans. Place dough in pans, cover, and let rise. Bake as described above and remove from pans when done, inverting buns onto plate and scraping mixture left in pans onto the buns.

Yield: 1½ dozen.

Judith A. Smith
Killingworth, Connecticut

Old-Fashioned Hot Cross Buns

ð

2 medium-size potatoes
½ cup milk
1 teaspoon salt
½ cup sugar
½ cup (1 stick) margarine
2 packages dry yeast
½ cup warm water
2 eggs
4½ cups unbleached all-purpose
  flour, sifted
Grated zest of 1 lemon
¾ cup raisins (rinsed with
  hot water and drained)
1 egg yolk
½ cup sifted confectioners' sugar

This recipe was given to me about 20 years ago when I lived in Canada. It never fails—the buns are always light and fluffy.

Peel and boil potatoes, drain, and mash until smooth. Scald milk and stir in salt, sugar, margarine, and ¾ cup mashed potatoes; cool to lukewarm.

In large bowl, sprinkle yeast on warm water and stir until dissolved. Add potato mixture and blend. Beat eggs slightly and add to yeast-and-potato mixture. Stir in half the flour and the lemon zest, beating until smooth.

Add remaining flour to make an easily handled dough. Turn onto lightly floured surface and knead until smooth and elastic, about 10 minutes. Place in greased bowl, grease surface of dough, cover with towel, and let rise in warm place until doubled in bulk.

Punch dough down, turn out onto lightly floured surface, and knead raisins into dough. Divide in half and roll both parts into cylinder shape about 12 inches long. With sharp knife, cut both into 12 equal pieces. Form into smooth balls and place on greased baking sheet about ¼ inch apart.

Beat egg yolk with 2 tablespoons water and brush over buns. Cover and set in warm place until doubled in bulk. Bake in preheated 375°F oven for about 25 minutes. Cool buns thoroughly.

Combine confectioners' sugar with enough water to form icing. Apply icing in cross shape, or spread over top of each bun.

Yield: 2 dozen.

Constance M. Ellway
Hailey, Idaho

BUTTERHORNS

ﻋ

1 cake yeast
1 tablespoon water
1 tablespoon sugar
1 cup lukewarm water
½ cup (1 stick) butter, melted
½ cup sugar
3 eggs, beaten
4 cups unbleached
   all-purpose flour
¼ teaspoon salt

Beautiful, luscious, feathery-light rolls (see page 129). My mother (four score and 12 years) made these regularly for at least 50 years. I treasure the recipe; it's an heirloom!

Crumble yeast in 1 tablespoon water combined with 1 tablespoon sugar. Add lukewarm water, cooled melted butter, ½ cup sugar, eggs, flour, and salt, mixing well. Place in greased bowl, grease top of dough, and refrigerate overnight.

Divide dough in half and roll out on floured surface about ¼-inch thick. Cut both portions into 16 wedges (as for pie) and roll up from wide end to tip. Place on greased baking sheets and let rise about 2 hours. Bake in preheated 400°F oven for 15 to 20 minutes, or until lightly browned.

Yield: 32 rolls.

Ellen Scannell
North Caldwell, New Jersey

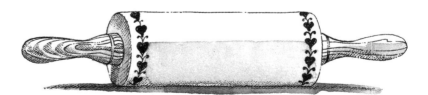

FABULOUS CRESCENT ROLLS

24

1 cup milk
¾ cup (1½ sticks) butter
¼ cup sugar
½ teaspoon salt
1 package dry yeast
¼ cup warm water
4 cups unbleached
  all-purpose flour
2 eggs
Melted butter for
  brushing on rolls

These rolls are as light as air and are a perfect companion to a traditional Thanksgiving dinner. They don't require kneading, and if you make them ahead of time and freeze them, you can serve delicious homemade rolls without any extra hassle on the big day.

Heat milk, butter, sugar, and salt in saucepan until butter melts, then set aside to cool. Dissolve yeast in warm water in large bowl of electric mixer. Beat cooled milk mixture into yeast mixture. Add 2 cups of the flour and beat at slow, then medium, speed for 2 minutes. Beat in eggs and slowly add 1 more cup flour, beating at low speed for 2 minutes. Stir in ¾ cup flour until smooth and elastic. Turn into oiled bowl and cover with warm, damp towel. Let rise until doubled in bulk.

Punch down. Divide dough into 4 equal pieces. Use remaining ¼ cup flour to dust surface and roll out each piece into 12-inch-diameter circle. Brush with melted butter. Cut into 8 wedges as though cutting a pie. Roll up from wide end to tip to form crescents, place on baking sheets, and brush with melted butter. Let rise until doubled in bulk.

Bake in preheated 400°F oven for 10 to 12 minutes, or until lightly browned. Cool on wire racks. Serve immediately or store in refrigerator or freezer. If frozen, arrange on baking sheet and heat at 350°F for about 15 minutes.

Yield: 32 rolls.

Sheila Eaton
Las Vegas, Nevada

Butterhorns, top, (page 127) and Oat Bran Rolls (page 148).

129

Date-Filled Cookies (page 86).

130

Chocolate Cake with Fluffy Coconut Frosting (page 46).

Black Forest Cheesecake (page 29).

Sinbad Bars, striped, (page 94) and Raspberry Bars (page 91).

Anne's Oatmeal Cookies, top, (page 71) and Kifle Cookies (page 84).

Orange-Chocolate Muffins (page 110) and Raspberry Honey Banana Muffins (page 103).

Peda Bread (page 188).

CHEESE CRESCENTS

ð

1 cup unbleached
  all-purpose flour
½ cup (1 stick) margarine,
  softened
1 cup farmer's cheese or
  well-drained cottage
  cheese, divided
½ teaspoon salt, divided
1 egg, beaten

These tender, flaky treats are a perfect accompaniment to a summer fruit salad or an elegant substitution for crackers and cheese when entertaining. Serve warm from the oven.

Mix flour, margarine, ½ cup of the cheese, and ¼ teaspoon salt until well blended. Divide dough into 3 balls, wrap individually in wax paper, and refrigerate for several hours or several days, until needed.

On floured surface, roll each into 10-inch circle about ⅛-inch thick. Cut into 8 wedges. Combine remaining ½ cup cheese, remaining ¼ teaspoon salt, and egg. Spoon ½ tablespoon of mixture on wide end of wedge and roll up from wide end to tip. Place on greased baking sheet, bend into crescent shape, and bake on top rack of preheated 400°F oven for 18 to 20 minutes. Remove and cool on rack.

Yield: 2 dozen.

Hilma McComb
Manchester, Connecticut

137

FAVORITE BUTTERMILK ROLLS

❧

2 packages dry yeast
¼ cup lukewarm water
3 tablespoons sugar, divided
1½ cups buttermilk
½ cup corn oil
4½ cups unbleached
   all-purpose flour
1 teaspoon salt
½ teaspoon baking soda
Melted margarine

These beautiful, flavorful rolls have a smooth, almost silky texture, and they are simple to make. What more could one ask for!

In large bowl, stir together yeast, water, and 1 tablespoon of the sugar; set aside. Heat buttermilk until lukewarm and combine with yeast mixture. Add remaining 2 tablespoons sugar and oil, and mix well. Sift together flour, salt, and soda, and stir into liquid ingredients, 2 cups at a time. Let stand for 10 minutes.

Turn out onto floured surface and knead for 5 minutes. Shape into rolls, place in greased pans, and brush with melted margarine. Let rise about 30 minutes, then bake in preheated 400°F oven for about 8 to 10 minutes.

Yield: 2 dozen 3-inch rolls.

Mrs. Joseph B. Denicola
Hartselle, Alabama

BUTTERMILK ROLLS

❧

2 packages dry yeast
4 tablespoons sugar, divided
¼ cup warm water
1 cup buttermilk
¼ cup (½ stick) butter
2 eggs at room temperature
5 cups bread flour
   (approximately)
2 teaspoons salt
1 egg beaten with
   1 tablespoon water
Poppy or sesame seeds

These flaky rolls are very professional looking and will be a hit at any party. They make a great gift and are sure to go quickly at bake sales.

Mix yeast and 1 tablespoon of the sugar in warm water until dissolved. Heat buttermilk until warm; add butter and remaining 3 tablespoons sugar, stirring to dissolve. Beat 2 eggs in large mixing bowl and add lukewarm buttermilk mixture and yeast mixture, stirring well. Combine flour and salt, and gradually mix into liquid ingredients.

Turn out onto floured surface and knead until smooth and elastic. Place dough in greased bowl and cover; let rise until doubled in bulk.

Punch down dough, shape into rolls, place in greased pans,

and let rise about 1 hour. Brush with egg-and-water mixture and sprinkle with poppy or sesame seeds. Bake in preheated 400°F oven for 10 minutes.

Yield: 2 dozen.

Vickie M. Townsend
Irmo, South Carolina

FEATHERBED ROLLS

ⱥ

1 cup milk
½ cup shortening
1 package dry yeast
¼ cup lukewarm water
1 egg, beaten
1½ tablespoons sugar
½ teaspoon salt
4 cups unbleached
    all-purpose flour (approximately)

Attractive, nicely risen, and light, these versatile rolls go with any meal and can even be used for small sandwiches. For a sweet, crusty top, brush with melted butter and sprinkle with brown sugar before baking.

In small saucepan, scald milk, add shortening, and stir until melted. Remove from heat and cool to lukewarm.

Sprinkle yeast in water to soften. Add to cooled milk mixture along with egg, sugar, salt, and 3 cups of the flour, beating well. Blend in additional 1 cup flour to make dough stiff enough to drop from a spoon. Cover and let rise about 1 hour.

Stir down dough and spoon into buttered muffin cups, filling them half full. Let rise until about doubled in size (30 to 60 minutes) and bake in preheated 400°F oven for 12 to 15 minutes.

Yield: 1½ dozen.

Doris Schwartz
Franksville, Wisconsin

SWEDISH ROLLS

&

2 cakes yeast
½ cup lukewarm water
2 eggs
1 cup lukewarm milk
4 cups unbleached
   all-purpose flour
½ cup granulated sugar
½ teaspoon salt
1 cup shortening
Confectioners' sugar
Almond extract
Ground black walnuts or
   hickory nuts

This is an old, secret recipe I've never given out until now—but for HARROWSMITH COUNTRY LIFE magazine, only my best! These are easy to mix, somewhat difficult to roll out because the dough is not kneaded, and exceedingly difficult to stop eating. They are very light and wonderfully flavored, yet not sugary sweet with tons of calories.

Dissolve yeast in lukewarm water. Beat eggs, combine with milk, and add to yeast mixture. In large bowl, combine flour, sugar, and salt, and cut in shortening until mixture resembles pie pastry. Add flour mixture to yeast mixture and blend well. Cover and refrigerate overnight.

Divide dough into 4 equal parts. On well-floured surface, roll each out to 10- or 12-inch circle. With long, sharp knife, press into dough, cutting into 8 wedges. (Dragging knife through dough makes edges ragged.) Roll up wedges from wide end to tip, place on lightly greased baking sheets, leaving 2 to 3 inches between rolls, and let rise until doubled in bulk, about 2 hours.

Bake in preheated 350°F oven for 12 to 15 minutes, or until light brown. While warm, frost with confectioners' sugar mixed with small amount of water and several drops of almond extract, and sprinkle with ground nuts.

Yield: 32 rolls.

Connie B. Webb
Paulding, Ohio

MOM'S EASY CINNAMON ROLLS

&

DOUGH
2 packages dry yeast
1 cup warm water
½ cup lard
½ cup sugar
2 teaspoons salt
1 cup hot water
2 eggs, beaten
6 cups unbleached
  all-purpose flour

CINNAMON ROLL FILLING
¾ cup (1½ sticks) butter, softened
1 cup granulated sugar
3 tablespoons cinnamon
Raisins
Confectioners' sugar

CINNAMON ROLL GOOEY
½ cup (1 stick) butter, melted
2 cups brown sugar
4 tablespoons white corn syrup
1 cup chopped nuts

Back on the farm when Mom baked bread every other day, she wanted a multipurpose recipe to save time. She came up with this, which she used for bread, cinnamon rolls, and even fried doughnuts. Now she uses it to bake huge batches of dinner rolls for family gatherings. These rolls are in such demand with the grandchildren and great-grandchildren that one grandson was moved to write the following poem: GRANDMA'S BUNS—"From coast to coast you can hear us boast/ Our Grandma's buns—they are the most!"

To make dough, dissolve yeast in warm water in small bowl. In large bowl, cream lard, sugar, and salt until smooth. Stir in hot water and cool to room temperature. Add yeast, eggs, and flour, blending well. Turn out onto floured surface and knead until shiny and smooth. Grease bowl, return dough to bowl, cover, and let rise 1 hour. Punch down and roll out for cinnamon rolls.

Combine filling ingredients, except for raisins and confectioners' sugar, and spread on rolled-out dough. Roll up, pinching seam to close, and slice into 24 pieces. Place 9 of the rolls in greased 9-inch square pan and sprinkle with raisins. Cover and let rise.

Make the gooey by mixing butter, brown sugar, and corn syrup. Pour into bottom of 9x13-inch pan and sprinkle with nuts. Place remaining 15 rolls on top, cover, and let rise.

When both pans of rolls have doubled in size, bake in preheated 350°F oven for 45 minutes. Immediately invert 9x13-inch pan onto serving plate or aluminum foil, scraping any of the gooey left in bottom of pan onto rolls. Let 9-inch square pan cool, then frost rolls with confectioners' sugar mixed with enough water to give consistency desired.

Yield: 2 dozen.

Betty Wicklein
Fort Dodge, Iowa

CARAMEL ROLLS

❧

2 packages dry yeast
½ cup warm water
½ cup lukewarm milk
½ cup sugar
1 teaspoon salt
2 eggs
½ cup (1 stick) butter, softened
4½ to 5 cups unbleached
  all-purpose flour

FILLING
1 to 2 tablespoons butter, softened
1 to 1½ teaspoons cinnamon
Confectioners' sugar to taste
2 to 3 tablespoons brown sugar

CARAMEL
½ cup brown sugar
4 tablespoons butter
¼ to ½ cup cream

This is a recipe my mother used to make frequently during the winter. They are absolutely decadent!

Dissolve yeast in warm water. Stir in milk, sugar, salt, eggs, butter, and 2½ cups of the flour, beating until smooth. Mix in enough remaining flour to make dough easy to handle.

Turn out onto lightly floured surface and knead until smooth and elastic, about 5 minutes. Place in greased bowl and rotate so that greased side is up. Cover and let rise until doubled in bulk, about 1½ hours.

Punch down dough, turn out onto lightly floured surface, and roll into 11x17-inch rectangle. Cover with filling ingredients by spreading with butter and sprinkling with cinnamon, confectioners' sugar, and brown sugar. Roll up like a jelly roll, beginning at long side, and cut into 18 slices, each about 1½ inches wide.

Prepare caramel by dividing brown sugar between two 9x13-inch pans and spreading over bottoms. Cut butter into pats and distribute over top of brown sugar in both pans, then pour cream over that. Place rolls in pans, leaving space in between for rising and to allow caramel to bubble up between them during baking. Cover, let rise until doubled in bulk, and bake in preheated 375°F oven for 25 to 30 minutes.

Yield: 1½ dozen.

B. J. Strong
Anchorage, Alaska

Orange Swirl Rolls

ે&

2 packages dry yeast
½ cup warm water
½ cup milk
½ cup sugar
½ cup (1 stick) margarine
1 teaspoon salt
4½ cups unbleached
    all-purpose flour
2 eggs, lightly beaten

FILLING/FROSTING
3 tablespoons butter, melted
2 tablespoons orange juice
1 tablespoon grated orange zest
1½ cups confectioners' sugar

These rolls make a delicious contribution to potluck brunches. They are easy, attractive, and distinctive, and can be made ahead and frozen.

Dissolve yeast in warm water. Scald milk, then add sugar, margarine, and salt, and allow to cool. Add flour, eggs, and yeast mixture, and blend well.

Turn out onto floured surface and knead for about 5 minutes, then transfer to large greased bowl. Allow to rise until doubled in bulk.

Combine filling ingredients until well blended. Turn out dough onto floured surface and roll out to about ¼-inch thickness. Spread with half the filling. Roll dough up tightly like a jelly roll and pinch seam to seal. Cut into 16 slices about ½-inch thick, place on greased baking sheet, and let rise until doubled. Bake in preheated 375°F oven for 25 minutes. Frost rolls with remaining filling as soon as they are removed from oven. Cool and remove from pan.

Yield: 16 rolls.

Constance M. Ellway
Hailey, Idaho

GLAZED ORANGE ROLLS

&

4 to 4½ cups unbleached
   all-purpose flour
1 tablespoon (1 package) dry yeast
Grated zest of 2 large oranges
   (about 3 tablespoons)
1 cup skim milk
½ cup sugar
½ teaspoon salt
3 tablespoons margarine
3 whole eggs (or 3 egg whites,
   if watching cholesterol)

FILLING

6 tablespoons margarine, softened
½ cup sugar
Grated zest of 2 large oranges
   (about 3 tablespoons)

GLAZE

1 cup sifted confectioners' sugar
2 to 3 tablespoons fresh
   orange juice

These citrusy, pretty, and delectable breakfast rolls are low in cholesterol if you use skim milk and egg whites. Although grating the zest and juicing the oranges is tedious and time-consuming, these ingredients make all the difference in flavor.

In large mixer bowl, combine 2 cups of the flour, yeast, and orange zest. Heat milk, sugar, salt, and margarine, stirring until warm (about 125°F on a cooking thermometer; it doesn't matter if margarine is not completely melted). Add to dry ingredients along with whole eggs or whites, and mix at low speed, then beat at high speed for about 3 minutes. By hand, stir in enough remaining flour to make a moderately soft dough.

Turn out onto floured surface and knead for about 5 minutes, or until dough is smooth. Cover and let rise until doubled in bulk.

While dough is rising, make filling by combining margarine, sugar, and orange zest, and beating until smooth.

Punch dough down, divide in half, and let rest for 10 minutes. On floured surface, roll each half into 8x12-inch rectangle about ¼-inch thick. Spread filling over both rectangles of dough and, starting from the long side, roll up tightly like a jelly roll. Cut both rolls into 1-inch-thick slices (for a total of 24 slices) and place each slice, cut side down, in greased muffin cup or 9-inch pie pan. Cover, place in warm spot, and let dough rise until doubled in bulk.

Bake in preheated 375°F oven for 15 to 17 minutes. For glaze, combine confectioners' sugar and orange juice and drizzle over rolls after they have cooled on rack.

Yield: 2 dozen.

Elizabeth Léonie Simpson
Woodside, California

144

SOUR-CREAM TWISTS

20

1 tablespoon (1 package) dry yeast
¼ cup lukewarm water
4 cups unbleached
  all-purpose flour
1 teaspoon salt
1 cup (2 sticks) butter
  or shortening
1 egg plus 2 yolks
1 cup sour cream
1 teaspoon vanilla
Sugar for sprinkling
  (about ¾ to 1 cup total)

If my family has a favorite recipe, this has to be it. I have been making these delicious pastrylike creations for more than 40 years, and now my sons are making them for their families. Habit-forming, to say the least!

Stir yeast into lukewarm water and set aside to soften. Sift flour and salt into large bowl and cut in butter as if making pie pastry. Beat egg and yolks together, and combine with sour cream, vanilla, and yeast. Add to flour mixture and blend thoroughly. Let rise in refrigerator for 2 hours or overnight.

Lightly sprinkle some of the sugar on flat surface and turn out dough. Lightly sprinkle more sugar over dough and roll out to 10- to 12-inch square. Sprinkle with more sugar and fold both sides of dough toward the center but without overlapping sides. Turn dough over, roll out again, and repeat folding procedure, using more sugar. Do this 4 times in all, sprinkling sugar on surface and on dough each time to prevent sticking.

Cut rolled-out dough into strips about ¾-inch wide and 4 inches long (and thin enough so twists aren't too thick). Roll each strip in sugar, twist, and lay on ungreased baking sheet several inches apart. (No additional rising is needed.) Bake in preheated 375°F oven for about 20 minutes, or until light brown. Watch carefully so sugar on bottom does not get too brown.

Yield: About 3 dozen.

*Phyllis DeHart Gray
Redway, California*

WHOLE-WHEAT ROLLS

ᥱ

2 tablespoons (2 packages)
  dry yeast
⅔ cup honey
1 cup warm water
½ cup oil
3 eggs
3¼ cups whole-wheat
  flour, divided
⅓ cup dry powdered milk
2 teaspoons salt

Easy to make, these whole-wheat rolls are surprisingly light and moist with just a hint of sweetness.

In large bowl, combine yeast, honey, and warm water, and let stand 5 minutes. Add oil, eggs, and 2½ cups of the flour; beat 100 strokes. Sift in remaining ¾ cup flour, dry powdered milk, and salt, blending thoroughly. Cover and let rise until doubled in bulk (about 1 hour). Stir down dough and let rise again, about 45 minutes.

Shape dough into 20 rolls and place side by side in greased pans. Bake in preheated 350°F oven for 20 to 25 minutes. Pull apart and serve warm with butter.

Yield: 20 rolls.

Joan Tuchman
San Francisco, California

RICH YEAST ROLLS

ᥱ

½ teaspoon sugar
¼ cup warm water
1 package dry yeast
2 eggs, beaten
¼ cup (½ stick) margarine,
  softened
¼ cup sugar
½ cup evaporated milk
½ cup warm water
4½ cups unbleached
  all-purpose flour
1¼ teaspoons salt

Rich yet light, with a lovely shape. I bake about 15 dozen of these rolls as Christmas care packages, and they have been taken all over the U.S. for Christmas dinner. My husband complains that we give them all away, but we really don't.

Combine ½ teaspoon sugar and ¼ cup warm water, and stir in yeast. Let rest about 5 to 10 minutes.

In large bowl, beat together eggs, margarine, ¼ cup sugar, milk, and ½ cup warm water. Add proofed yeast, 2½ cups of the flour, and salt, beating at medium speed for 5 minutes. Add remaining 2 cups flour and beat until satiny. Cover and let rest 10 minutes.

Turn dough out onto floured surface and knead 10 to 12 minutes. Place in greased bowl and rotate to grease all sides. Cover and let rise until doubled in bulk.

(continued)

Punch down dough, turn out onto floured surface, and divide into 24 pieces, shaping into balls. Place in well-greased round cake pans and let rise until doubled, about 40 minutes. Bake in preheated 400°F oven for 15 to 20 minutes.

Yield: 2 dozen.

Mrs. A. L. Britz
Encinitas, California

MASHED-POTATO REFRIGERATOR ROLLS

֍

1 package dry yeast
½ cup lukewarm water
1 cup smooth mashed potatoes
⅔ cup shortening
½ cup sugar
½ teaspoon salt
1 cup milk, scalded
2 eggs, well beaten
4 cups sifted unbleached
   all-purpose flour
   (approximately)

This recipe, using leftover mashed potatoes, has been handed down in my family for five generations. The greatest thing about it is that you can make the dough ahead and it will keep in the refrigerator for a week or more. This way you can enjoy hot rolls every day.

Dissolve yeast in water and set aside to soften. In large bowl, combine mashed potatoes, shortening, sugar, salt, and scalded milk, mixing well.

Stir yeast and eggs into cooled potato mixture. Gradually add enough flour to make a stiff dough. Turn out onto floured surface and knead well for 5 to 8 minutes. Place in greased bowl, grease top of dough, and cover tightly. Store in refrigerator until ready to use.

About an hour before serving, shape dough into small balls and place 3 in each cup of greased muffin tins to make cloverleaf rolls. Let rise, then bake in preheated 425°F oven for 10 minutes, or until light brown.

Yield: 2 dozen.

Carole Leamon
Sebring, Florida

Oat-Bran Rolls

ช•

1 cup oat bran
2⅓ cups water, divided
3 tablespoons margarine
3 tablespoons sugar
1½ teaspoons salt
2 packages dry yeast
4 to 6 cups unbleached
  all-purpose flour
Milk or melted butter (optional)
Oats or oat bran for
  sprinkling tops (optional)

These rolls are nice and moist, and they keep for several days (see page 129). They also freeze well. Cooking the oat bran makes the rolls softer and lighter than they would be if dry oat bran was added along with the flour. You can replace the oat bran with an equal amount of rolled oats, if you wish, and cook as directed.

In microwave, cook oat bran in 2 cups of the water for about 3 or 4 minutes on high, or until mixture starts to boil. (Mixture should be thick.) Remove from microwave, add margarine, sugar, and salt, and stir to blend. Set aside to cool to 125°F.

Heat remaining ⅓ cup water to 125°F and add yeast, stirring to dissolve. Add to oat-bran mixture and stir. Begin stirring in flour gradually, and as dough gets stiff, turn out onto floured surface and knead for 5 to 8 minutes, or until smooth and elastic, adding more flour if needed. Place dough in greased bowl, rotate to grease top, cover, and let rise in warm place until doubled in bulk, about 1 hour.

Punch dough down and shape into small balls. For cloverleaf shape, place 3 balls in each cup of greased muffin tins, cover, and let rise until doubled. Brush lightly with milk or melted butter and sprinkle with oats or oat bran, if desired. Bake in preheated 350°F oven for 20 to 30 minutes. Cool on racks.

Yield: 2 dozen.

Carol Forcum
Marion, Illinois

GOLDEN ONION ROLLS

2 packages dry yeast
½ cup warm water
¼ cup sugar
¼ cup shortening
1 tablespoon salt
  (or less to taste)
¾ cup milk, scalded
2 eggs
5 to 5½ cups sifted unbleached
  all-purpose flour

ONION FILLING
2 cups chopped onions
  (about 2 to 3)
¼ cup (½ stick) butter
¼ teaspoon salt
2 tablespoons cream
2 tablespoons slightly beaten egg
  (reserve remainder)
Poppy or sesame seeds

This recipe has won many blue ribbons at the county and state fairs. You can reduce the amount of salt used in the dough, if desired, but be sure to use an ample 2 cups of onions in the filling.

Stir yeast into warm water and set aside to soften. In separate bowl, combine sugar, shortening, salt, and hot, scalded milk. Stir to melt shortening and cool to lukewarm.

Blend eggs with softened yeast and stir into cooled milk mixture. Gradually add flour to form a stiff dough.

Turn dough out onto floured surface and knead until smooth and satiny, about 3 to 5 minutes. Place in greased bowl, cover, and let rise in warm place until light and doubled in size, about 1 hour.

Meanwhile, prepare the filling. Saute onions in butter in saucepan until golden in color. Remove from heat and add salt, cream, and slightly beaten egg, stirring thoroughly. Set aside to cool.

Shape dough into 2-inch balls and place on greased baking sheets. Flatten, press thumb in center of each ball to form a hollow, and spoon in a tablespoonful of filling. Brush rolls with remaining beaten egg and sprinkle with poppy or sesame seeds. Let rise until light and doubled in size, about 45 minutes.

Bake in preheated 400°F oven for 12 to 16 minutes, or until golden brown.

Yield: About 2 dozen.

Sue Jones
Springfield, Missouri

QUICK BREADS

QUICK CINNAMON BREAD

ಎ

2 cups unbleached
   all-purpose flour
¾ cup sugar
1½ teaspoons cinnamon
4 teaspoons baking powder
½ teaspoon salt
2 teaspoons vanilla
2 eggs
⅓ cup oil
1 cup buttermilk (or
   1 tablespoon vinegar
   mixed with 1 cup milk)

STREUSEL TOPPING
2 tablespoons sugar
2 teaspoons cinnamon
2 teaspoons margarine, softened

A fine brunch or tea bread dressed up with a streusel topping. Ideal for spur-of-the-moment occasions, unexpected company, or a midday urge for something sweet.

In large bowl, combine flour, sugar, cinnamon, baking powder, salt, vanilla, eggs, oil, and buttermilk. Beat until thoroughly blended. Pour batter into greased and floured 9-inch loaf pan.

Combine streusel ingredients, sprinkle over top of batter, and swirl in lightly with knife. Bake in preheated 350°F oven for 45 minutes, or until toothpick inserted in center comes out clean. Remove from pan and cool before slicing.

Yield: One 9-inch loaf.

Sandra Sue Rooker
Mason, Michigan

APRICOT BREAD

ja.

½ cup dried apricots
1 large orange
½ cup raisins
½ cup chopped almonds
2 cups unbleached
  all-purpose flour
2 teaspoons baking powder
1 teaspoon baking soda
1 cup sugar
¼ teaspoon salt
1 egg, lightly beaten
2 tablespoons butter, melted
1 teaspoon vanilla

Chopped apricots, orange zest, and raisins provide color as well as a pleasing texture. This is a great recipe to make in small gift-size loaves for the holidays.

Cover apricots with water and soak ½ hour. Squeeze juice from orange, save rind, and add enough boiling water to juice to make 1 cup. Set aside.

Drain apricots and transfer to food chopper or food processor along with orange rind and raisins. Process until finely chopped. (Or grate orange rind before juicing, chop apricots in processor, and keep raisins whole.) Combine with almonds in large bowl.

Sift flour, baking powder, soda, sugar, and salt over fruit and nuts, and mix well. Beat together orange juice, egg, cooled melted butter, and vanilla, and add to dry ingredients, mixing just until moistened. Pour into greased 9-inch loaf pan and bake in preheated 350°F oven for 1 hour, or until bread tests done.

Yield: One 9-inch loaf.

Jaine Parry
Apple Valley, Minnesota

APRICOT-RAISIN-BRAN BREAD

ja.

¾ cup coarsely chopped
  dried apricots
½ cup raisins
1 cup boiling water
(continued)

This bread is wonderful toasted and spread with butter. I like incorporating the unprocessed bran because it creates a nutty flavor, enhances the texture, and adds heartiness.

Combine apricots and raisins, pour in enough boiling water to cover them slightly, and let sit for 10 minutes. Drain well, add 3 tablespoons sugar, and stir to blend. Set aside.

Combine remaining ½ cup sugar with oil and beat well. Beat in eggs, one at a time, until thoroughly blended. Sift flour, baking powder, and salt together, and add alternately

3 tablespoons plus ½ cup sugar
⅓ cup oil
2 eggs
2¼ cups unbleached
    all-purpose flour
1 tablespoon baking powder
½ teaspoon salt
⅔ cup milk
¾ cup unprocessed bran

with milk and bran to the oil mixture. Fold in reserved fruits. Pour mixture into greased 8½-inch loaf pan and bake in preheated 350°F oven for 1 hour, or until cake tester comes out clean. Remove from oven and cool 10 minutes, then remove from pan and let cool completely on rack.

Yield: One 8½-inch loaf.

Victoria Palmer
Greenfield, Massachusetts

BANANA & SOUR-CREAM BREAD

25

2 large or 3 small
    ripe bananas
½ cup sour cream
1 teaspoon baking soda
1 teaspoon vanilla
¾ cup sugar
½ cup (1 stick) butter or
    margarine, softened
2 eggs
2 cups unbleached
    all-purpose flour
¼ teaspoon salt
1 teaspoon baking powder
1½ cups chopped walnuts
    (optional)

This is my Grandma Pearl's recipe—with some family alterations. She felt it was very important to mix the bananas, sour cream, soda, and vanilla together first and then let it sit—the longer the better, she said. She used sour milk; my mother changed this to sour cream and increased the amount from 1 tablespoon to ½ cup. Whenever I make this, my husband insists on the addition of walnuts.

On large plate or in shallow bowl, mash bananas with sour cream, soda, and vanilla. Cover with plastic wrap and let sit about half an hour or (if refrigerated) longer.

In large bowl, cream sugar and butter, add eggs, and beat until well blended. Add banana mixture and sift in flour, salt, and baking powder, stirring to combine. Mix in walnuts, if using. Pour into 1 greased 9-inch or 2 greased 7-inch loaf pans and bake in preheated 325°F oven for 30 to 45 minutes, or until toothpick inserted in middle comes out clean.

Yield: One 9-inch or two 7-inch loaves.

Joanne Pyc
Ozark, Missouri

FRESH GINGER BANANA BREAD

❧

½ cup (1 stick) butter, softened
½ cup granulated sugar
¼ cup packed brown sugar
2 eggs
2¼ cups unbleached all-purpose flour
2 teaspoons baking powder
½ teaspoon baking soda
½ teaspoon salt
1½ tablespoons peeled and minced fresh ginger
1 tablespoon fresh lemon juice
½ teaspoon grated lemon zest
2 medium-size ripe bananas, mashed
¼ cup plain nonfat yogurt
½ cup finely chopped walnuts

Fresh ginger turns ordinary banana bread into a delectable and unique treat. I love this sliced and toasted, or grilled in a small amount of butter.

Cream butter and sugars until smooth. Add eggs, one at a time, and beat until fluffy. In separate bowl, sift together flour, baking powder, soda, and salt. Combine fresh ginger, lemon juice, lemon zest, bananas, yogurt, and nuts, and mix well. Alternately add dry ingredients and ginger mixture to creamed mixture, beating thoroughly.

Pour into greased 9-inch loaf pan and bake in preheated 350°F oven for 50 to 55 minutes, or until bread tests done.

Yield: One 9-inch loaf.

Diane Taylor
Houston, Texas

POPPY-SEED BREAD

❧

3 cups unbleached all-purpose flour
1 cup sugar
1½ teaspoons baking powder
½ teaspoon salt
2 tablespoons poppy seeds
3 eggs
1½ cups skim milk
½ cup oil
1½ teaspoons vanilla
1½ teaspoons almond extract
(continued)

A rich, sweet, old-fashioned bread—old-fashioned because it reminds me of my great-grandmother Honey, who was an exceptionally fine baker and often used poppy seeds in sweet breads and rolls.

In large bowl, combine flour, sugar, baking powder, salt, and poppy seeds. Beat together eggs, milk, oil, vanilla, and almond extract, then stir into dry ingredients, mixing thoroughly.

Pour into 2 greased and floured 7-inch loaf pans and bake in preheated 350°F oven for 30 to 45 minutes. Cool in pans for 10 minutes, then turn out and cool completely.

To make the glaze, beat together confectioners' sugar, orange

GLAZE
1 cup sifted
  confectioners' sugar
2 tablespoons orange juice
¼ teaspoon vanilla
¼ teaspoon almond extract

juice, vanilla, and almond extract until smooth. Drizzle over cooled bread.

Yield: Two 7-inch loaves.

Candice Byerly
San Antonio, Texas

DATE-NUT BREAD

೭ఎ

1 cup sugar
1 cup chopped dates
1 cup water
1½ cups unbleached
  all-purpose flour
1 teaspoon baking soda
1 tablespoon margarine,
  softened
1 egg
½ cup chopped walnuts

This quick bread has been a holiday tradition with my family ever since my mother-in-law gave me the recipe years ago. Rich with dates, it always turns out nice and moist.

Combine sugar, dates, and water in saucepan and bring to a boil, stirring. Set aside to cool.

Mix flour and soda together in small bowl, then measure one-quarter of this mixture into large bowl and beat with margarine and egg until well blended. Mix in cooled date paste, then remaining flour and soda mixture, stirring to combine. Add nuts. Pour into greased 7-inch loaf pan and bake in preheated 350°F oven for 45 to 60 minutes.

Yield: One 7-inch loaf.

Jane McLean
Bemidji, Minnesota

make 6 min

CHERRY BREAD

৯

½ cup sugar

¾ cup oil

2 eggs

1 teaspoon vanilla

1½ cups unbleached
   all-purpose flour

1 teaspoon baking powder

1 teaspoon baking soda

¼ teaspoon nutmeg

½ teaspoon cinnamon

¼ teaspoon salt

1 cup sweet or sour cherries
   (bottled or canned), drained

¼ cup chopped nuts

If using maraschino cherries, you may want to reduce the sugar to ¼ cup or eliminate it altogether. For best results, let the bread sit for 24 hours before serving. Our recipe tester took this to her office to share with her co-workers and reported that it was "overwhelmingly praised and consumed in no time."

Beat together sugar, oil, eggs, and vanilla. In separate bowl, combine flour, baking powder, soda, nutmeg, cinnamon, and salt. Stir in egg mixture and add cherries and nuts, mixing lightly.

Pour into greased 9-inch loaf pan and bake in preheated 350°F oven for 55 to 60 minutes, or until bread tests done. Let cool for at least 10 minutes before removing from pan.

Yield: One 9-inch loaf.

Judy Stanton
Thompsonville, Michigan

LEMON TEA BREAD

৯

½ cup (1 stick) margarine (or
   ¼ cup butter and ¼ cup
   shortening), softened

1 cup sugar

2 eggs

Grated zest of 1 lemon

1½ cups unbleached
   all-purpose flour

1½ teaspoons baking powder

Pinch of salt (optional)

½ cup milk

(continued)

Moist and lemony—a bit like pound cake. Serve the bread chilled and thinly sliced.

Cream together margarine and sugar until light. Add eggs, one at a time, beating well after each addition. Stir in lemon zest. Sift together flour, baking powder, and salt, if using. Add milk and flour mixture alternately to creamed mixture, stirring until well blended. Turn into well-greased 9-inch loaf pan and bake in preheated 350°F oven for 45 to 50 minutes, or until loaf springs back when lightly touched.

Combine syrup ingredients, stirring until sugar is dissolved. Pierce top of hot loaf with tines of fork and pour syrup over cake. Let stand 10 minutes before turning out of pan.

(continued)

LEMON SYRUP
Grated zest and juice of
  1 lemon
¼ cup sugar

Wrap in foil and chill.

Yield: One 9-inch loaf.

Patricia Kerecz   *J. Elizabeth Fraser*
La Habra, California   *and*   *Sackville, New Brunswick, Canada*

MORNING-GLORY BREAD

❧

½ cup granulated sugar
¼ cup packed brown sugar
½ cup (1 stick) margarine or
  butter, softened
3 eggs
2 teaspoons vanilla
1½ cups unbleached
  all-purpose flour
½ cup wheat bran
2 teaspoons baking powder
1 teaspoon cinnamon
½ teaspoon salt
1½ cups grated carrots
1 cup peeled, cored, and
  chopped apples
½ cup golden raisins, softened
  in hot water and drained
½ cup chopped nuts (walnuts or
  pecans or mixture)
½ cup shredded coconut

This quick bread is jam-packed with nutritious ingredients and makes an appealing addition to breakfast as well as a late-night snack.

In large bowl, cream sugars and margarine until smooth and light. Add eggs, one at a time, beating well after each addition. Stir in vanilla. In separate bowl, combine flour, bran, baking powder, cinnamon, and salt. Add carrots, apples, raisins, nuts, and coconut, and toss to combine thoroughly. Stir into creamed mixture, blending well.

Spoon into greased 9-inch loaf pan and bake in preheated 325°F oven for 1 hour, or until bread tests done.

Yield: One 9-inch loaf.

Kenneth and Mia Burton
Ithaca, New York

CRANBERRY DATE-NUT BREAD

&

1 cup whole-wheat flour
1½ cups unbleached
   all-purpose flour
1 teaspoon baking powder
1 teaspoon baking soda
½ teaspoon salt
⅓ cup sugar
1 cup chopped dates
1 cup fresh cranberries
1 tablespoon grated orange zest
½ cup chopped pecans
1 tablespoon margarine, melted
2 egg whites
1 teaspoon vanilla
1 cup orange juice (or juice
   from 1 orange with enough
   water added to make 1 cup)

An attractive loaf with an excellent combination of flavors. Enjoyable any time of day—or night!

In large bowl, combine flours, baking powder, soda, salt, and sugar. Stir in fruits, zest, and nuts. In medium bowl, beat together cooled margarine, egg whites, vanilla, and juice, and mix well. Add wet ingredients to dry ingredients and stir until just moistened. Pour into greased 9-inch loaf pan and bake in preheated 325°F oven for about 1 hour.

Yield: One 9-inch loaf.

Rita Lyons
Port Orchard, Washington

CRANBERRY BREAD WITH CREAM CHEESE

❧

1 package (8 ounces)
   cream cheese, softened
1 cup (2 sticks) butter, softened
1½ cups granulated sugar
1½ teaspoons vanilla
4 eggs
2¼ cups sifted unbleached
   all-purpose flour
1½ teaspoons baking powder
2 cups fresh cranberries
½ cup chopped walnuts
1½ cups sifted confectioners' sugar
2 tablespoons milk

I got this years ago from a friend in Wisconsin, who said it was an award-winning recipe. I make it every Thanksgiving and Christmas—everyone loves it!

Blend together cream cheese, butter, granulated sugar, and vanilla until light. Add eggs, one at a time, beating well after each addition. Gradually add 2 cups of the flour sifted with baking powder. Toss remaining ¼ cup flour with cranberries and nuts, and fold into batter. Pour into 2 well-greased 9-inch loaf pans and bake in preheated 350°F oven for 1 hour and 20 minutes.

Combine confectioners' sugar and milk, and drizzle over bread while still warm.

Yield: Two 9-inch loaves.

Celia Taft
Huntington, West Virginia

CRANBERRY-ORANGE BREAD

❧

1½ cups unbleached
   all-purpose flour
½ cup whole-wheat pastry flour
1½ teaspoons baking powder
½ teaspoon baking soda
1 teaspoon salt
2 teaspoons cinnamon
½ teaspoon cloves
1 cup halved fresh cranberries
½ cup chopped walnuts
¾ cup orange juice
1 tablespoon grated orange zest
1 egg
2 tablespoons oil

Unusual and nutritious, this bread is dark, dense, and not at all sweet. Our recipe tester said she much preferred it with Thanksgiving turkey than the more traditional kind that is sweeter and "whiter."

Combine flours, baking powder, soda, salt, and spices. Stir in cranberries and nuts, and mix well. In separate bowl, beat together orange juice, zest, egg, and oil. Stir into flour-and-cranberry mixture, and blend. Spoon into greased and floured 9-inch loaf pan. Bake in preheated 350°F oven for about 50 minutes, or until toothpick inserted in center comes out clean.

Yield: One 9-inch loaf.

Kelly A. Murphy
Natchez, Mississippi

ORANGE NUT BREAD

❧

¾ cup sugar
½ cup (1 stick) margarine, softened
2 eggs
2 cups unbleached all-purpose flour
2 teaspoons baking powder
½ teaspoon salt
⅔ cup water
1 tablespoon grated orange zest
4 tablespoons fresh orange juice
⅓ cup chopped walnuts tossed lightly with flour

This is a very versatile recipe. I've replaced orange with lemon, grapefruit, or tangerine, all with equally fine results. Make a loaf of each for parties. The bread can be frozen, although there is some loss of flavor.

In large bowl, cream sugar and margarine. Add eggs, one at a time, and beat well. Sift together flour, baking powder, and salt, and stir into creamed mixture. Add water, orange zest, and orange juice, and stir to blend. Fold in walnuts. Pour into greased 9-inch loaf pan and bake in preheated 350°F oven for 50 minutes, or until bread tests done.

Yield: One 9-inch loaf.

Kristin E. Glick-Nuckolls
Elgin, Illinois

CARROT-NUT BREAD

❧

¾ cup oil
¾ cup sugar
2 eggs, beaten
1 teaspoon vanilla
1 cup unbleached all-purpose flour
½ cup whole-wheat flour
½ teaspoon salt
1 teaspoon baking powder
1 teaspoon baking soda
½ teaspoon cinnamon
½ teaspoon freshly grated nutmeg
1 cup grated carrots
1 cup chopped nuts

Nicely shaped, dark golden-brown loaves that hold together well. Substantial and not too oily. Serve with breakfast or as a snack.

In large bowl, beat together oil, sugar, eggs, and vanilla. Combine flours, salt, baking powder, soda, cinnamon, and nutmeg, and add to oil mixture, blending well. Stir in carrots and nuts. Pour into greased 9-inch loaf pan and bake in preheated 325°F oven for about 45 minutes, or until bread tests done. Turn out onto rack and cool thoroughly before cutting.

Yield: One 9-inch loaf.

Vickie M. Townsend
Irmo, South Carolina

SHERRY PUMPKIN BREAD

ò⁄

½ cup oil
1 cup brown sugar
2 eggs
1 cup cooked, mashed pumpkin
1 teaspoon cinnamon
½ teaspoon nutmeg
⅓ cup sherry
1 cup unbleached
   all-purpose flour
1 cup stone-ground
   whole-wheat flour
1 tablespoon baking powder
1 teaspoon salt
1 cup chopped nuts

I am going to miss making this bread for our boss, who passed away last summer. I can still see the big smile on his face whenever I handed him a loaf of this warm bread. He was 77 years old. We worked on his farm, and I also cooked for his hunters, for 22 years.

In large bowl, beat together oil, brown sugar, eggs, pumpkin, cinnamon, nutmeg, and sherry. In separate bowl, combine flours, baking powder, salt, and nuts. Add to wet ingredients and mix well.

Pour into 2 greased 9-inch loaf pans and bake in preheated 350°F oven for 30 minutes, or until top springs back when pressed with fingers. Cool 10 minutes, then remove from pans.

Yield: Two 9-inch loaves.

Mary Detweiler
West Farmington, Ohio

STRAWBERRY BREAD

ò⁄

3 cups unbleached
   all-purpose flour
1 teaspoon salt
2 cups sugar
1 teaspoon baking soda
3 teaspoons cinnamon
1¼ cups chopped nuts
4 eggs
1¼ cups oil
2 packages (10 ounces each)
   frozen, unsweetened
   strawberries, thawed

This is a great dessert bread that can be prepared ahead of time and frozen until needed. It is moist, spicy, and nutty, and can also be made, of course, with fresh strawberries.

Mix together flour, salt, sugar, soda, cinnamon, and nuts. In separate bowl, beat eggs and oil. Make well in dry ingredients, add combined eggs and oil, and mix gently. Fold in strawberries. Pour into 2 greased and floured 9-inch loaf pans and bake in preheated 350°F oven for 60 to 70 minutes, or until toothpick inserted in center comes out clean.

Yield: Two 9-inch loaves.   makes 6 mini

Joan Fields
Stoughton, Wisconsin

RHUBARB BREAD

&

1½ cups brown sugar
⅔ cup oil
1 egg
2½ cups unbleached
    all-purpose flour
1 teaspoon salt
1 teaspoon baking soda
1 cup buttermilk
1 teaspoon vanilla
2 cups diced rhubarb
    (if frozen, thaw in colander
    and press out excess liquid)
½ cup coarsely chopped
    walnuts (optional)

TOPPING
½ cup granulated sugar
1 teaspoon cinnamon
1 tablespoon butter, softened

Of the many ways I use rhubarb, this is by far the easiest and most popular at our house. The tartness of the rhubarb contrasts nicely with the sweetness of the bread and its spicy topping. This is a moist and attractive bread.

Beat together brown sugar, oil, and egg. Sift flour, salt, and soda, and stir into brown-sugar mixture, alternating with buttermilk. Add vanilla and blend well. Stir in rhubarb and nuts, if using. Spoon into 2 well-greased and floured 8-inch loaf pans.

Combine topping ingredients until thoroughly blended, then sprinkle over each loaf. Bake in preheated 325°F oven for 40 to 50 minutes, or until toothpick inserted in center comes out clean. Cool in pans 10 minutes; remove from pans and cool on racks.

Yield: Two 8-inch loaves.

*Adeline Halfmann
Campbellsport, Wisconsin*

ORANGE ZUCCHINI BREAD

๛

1 cup unbleached
  all-purpose flour
1 teaspoon baking powder
½ teaspoon baking soda
¼ teaspoon salt
1 teaspoon cinnamon
½ teaspoon nutmeg
¾ cup sugar (or less if bran
  cereal contains sugar)
½ cup oil
2 eggs
½ cup bran cereal
1½ teaspoons grated orange zest
1 teaspoon vanilla
1 cup grated zucchini
½ cup chopped or ground nuts

ORANGE CREAM GLAZE
1½ ounces cream cheese, softened
1 tablespoon margarine, melted
½ teaspoon grated orange zest
¾ cup confectioners' sugar
1 tablespoon water
1 teaspoon milk

This has a lot of ingredients, but it's worth the effort, for everyone tells me it's their favorite recipe for zucchini bread. I make several batches at one time and freeze the extra loaves. Good for breakfast, snacks, and desserts, and helps get a handle on that zucchini crop!

Combine flour, baking powder, soda, salt, cinnamon, and nutmeg. Set aside. In large mixing bowl, beat sugar, oil, and eggs until well blended. Stir in cereal, orange zest, and vanilla. Add flour mixture, zucchini, and nuts, stirring until well blended. Spoon into greased 9-inch loaf pan and bake in preheated 325°F oven for 40 minutes, or until toothpick inserted near center comes out clean.

While bread is cooling, blend ingredients for glaze, adjusting amounts to suit taste and for desired consistency. Pour glaze over still-warm bread.

Yield: One 9-inch loaf.

Lula Bowling
Pikeville, Kentucky

CHOCOLATE ZUCCHINI BREAD

❧

3 eggs
½ cup sour cream or
  plain yogurt
1¾ cups sugar
1⅔ cups oil
2½ cups grated zucchini
4 teaspoons vanilla
2¾ cups sifted unbleached
  all-purpose flour
½ cup oats
1½ teaspoons salt
2 teaspoons baking powder
2 teaspoons baking soda
1 tablespoon cinnamon
5 heaping tablespoons cocoa
1¼ cups chopped walnuts
1 cup raisins

"Chocolate WHAT bread?" my co-workers asked me after biting into my latest concoction. You wouldn't believe there's any zucchini in it at all—but there is! Finding a use for a bushel of fresh zucchini per week forces one to be creative. This bread is great as a breakfast treat or as an elegant dessert with vanilla ice cream. Real chocoholics—like me—will add hot-fudge sauce on top.

In large mixing bowl, beat eggs on high speed for about 1 minute. On medium speed, beat in sour cream, sugar, oil, zucchini, and vanilla. On low speed, add flour, oats, salt, baking powder, soda, cinnamon, and cocoa, blending well. Stir in walnuts and raisins on low speed, or by hand. Pour into 2 greased 9-inch loaf pans and bake in preheated 350°F oven for 50 to 65 minutes, or until bread tests done. Cool 10 minutes, then turn out onto racks to cool completely.

Yield: Two 9-inch loaves.

Elizabeth G. Lloyd
Gaithersburg, Maryland

ZUCCHINI BREAD

৯

3 eggs
1½ cups sugar
1 cup oil
1 tablespoon vanilla
4 teaspoons lemon juice or
    vinegar
2 cups grated zucchini, unpeeled
2 cups unbleached
    all-purpose flour
1 cup whole-wheat flour
1 teaspoon salt
1 teaspoon baking soda
½ teaspoon baking powder
1 tablespoon cinnamon
1 cup chopped walnuts
½ to 1 cup raisins, soaked in
    boiling water to cover, drained

I use part whole-wheat flour to increase the nutritional value of this bread. The lemon juice or vinegar neutralizes the soda and gives a better rise, removing any soda taste, too. The bread is moist and delicious, and also freezes well.

Beat eggs until light and fluffy. Slowly add sugar while continuing to beat. Stir in oil, vanilla, and lemon juice or vinegar. Add zucchini and mix thoroughly. Sift together flours, salt, soda, baking powder, and cinnamon, and stir into zucchini mixture just until moistened. Fold in nuts and raisins. Pour into 2 greased 8-inch loaf pans and bake in preheated 325°F oven for 1 hour.

Yield: Two 8-inch loaves.

Betty Clifton
Three Rivers, Michigan

GRAPE-NUTS BREAD

৯

½ cup Grape-Nuts cereal
1 cup sour milk (1 cup milk
    mixed with 1 tablespoon
    vinegar)
1 egg, beaten
1½ cups unbleached
    all-purpose flour
½ teaspoon salt
½ teaspoon baking powder
½ teaspoon baking soda
½ cup sugar

My mother got this recipe during the Second World War. It was popular because it uses no shortening and little sugar— both of which were in short supply at that time. It was a family favorite when I was little and continued to be while my own children grew up.

Soak Grape-Nuts in milk for 20 minutes. Add egg and blend well. Sift together flour, salt, baking powder, soda, and sugar, and stir into Grape-Nuts mixture. Pour into greased and floured 7-inch loaf pan and bake in preheated 325°F oven for 50 minutes.

Yield: One 7-inch loaf.

Patricia Cavanaugh
Groton, New York

GRANDMA'S OATMEAL BREAD

❧

2 cups hot water
2 cups quick-cooking oats
1 cup (2 sticks) butter or margarine
3½ cups packed brown sugar
4 eggs, beaten
2 cups unbleached all-purpose flour
2 teaspoons baking soda
¼ teaspoon nutmeg
½ teaspoon cinnamon
1 cup raisins (optional)
1 cup chopped nuts (optional)

A sweet and substantial quick bread. To make this for breakfast, we suggest including the raisins and reducing the brown sugar to 1 cup, or less to taste.

In large bowl, pour hot water over oats and butter, stir to combine, and set aside for ½ hour. Cream brown sugar and eggs until light. Combine flour, soda, nutmeg, cinnamon, raisins (if using), and nuts (if using), and stir into creamed mixture. Add to oats and blend well. Pour into 2 greased and floured 9-inch loaf pans and bake in preheated 325°F oven for 1 hour.

Yield: Two 9-inch loaves.

Lynn Clubb
What Cheer, Iowa

IRISH FRECKLE BREAD

❧

4 cups unbleached all-purpose flour
¼ cup sugar
1 teaspoon salt
1 teaspoon baking powder
¼ cup (½ stick) margarine
2 cups raisins
1½ cups buttermilk
1 egg, beaten
1 teaspoon baking soda

Easy and unusual, this quick bread is similar to a biscuit or scone with its crumbly texture and not-too-sweet flavor. It's fantastic warm with butter and marmalade, or as an accompaniment to a nice, thick beef, carrot, and onion stew.

Sift together flour, sugar, salt, and baking powder. Cut in margarine until consistency resembles coarse cornmeal. Stir in raisins. Combine buttermilk, egg, and soda, and stir into dry mixture until just moist. Spoon into greased 8½-inch loaf pan, cut gash across the top in form of a cross, and bake in preheated 375°F oven for 45 to 50 minutes, or until brown. Cool on rack before cutting.

Yield: One 8½-inch loaf.

Dorothy Firchau
Lewisville, Minnesota

166

ALICE'S BROWN BREAD

ও

2 cups sour milk (2 cups milk
    mixed with 2 tablespoons
    vinegar or lemon juice)
2 eggs, beaten
2 tablespoons butter, melted
¼ cup molasses
5 cups graham or
    whole-wheat flour
½ cup sugar
½ teaspoon salt
1 teaspoon baking soda
1 cup raisins (optional)

In 1927, I attended my first wedding, with relatives and friends gathered in a Minnesota farmhouse. No catering then, but everyone, mindful of the quantities of food needed for so large a group, brought their best baking and cooking. My mother came home with this recipe, which she always called Alice's Brown Bread and baked often. Some adjustments were made over the years as the recipe moved from farm to city. For example, there always was sour milk on the farm; now I have to add lemon juice or vinegar to sweet milk (it's not the same). Molasses on the farm was always dark; today, I sometimes use light; graham flour has become stone-ground whole-wheat. I still bake this frequently and each time am impressed at how delicious so simple a recipe can be. Raisins are a delicious addition to this bread, which is surprisingly light, not heavy or dense as are many made entirely from whole-wheat flour. I am submitting the recipe because I have never seen it in any cookbook, and it is too good a bread to be lost.

Beat together sour milk, eggs, cooled melted butter, and molasses. Combine flour, sugar, salt, soda, and raisins (if using), and stir into milk mixture. Pour into greased 10½-inch loaf pan and bake in preheated 350°F oven for about 1 hour, or until center tests done.

Yield: One 10½-inch loaf.

Ruth M. Knott
Cleveland Heights, Ohio

BUTTERMILK-HERB-TOMATO BREAD

❧

2⅔ cups whole-wheat
　pastry flour
1 teaspoon baking powder
1 teaspoon baking soda
2 teaspoons crushed dried basil
1 teaspoon crushed dried thyme
¼ teaspoon freshly ground
　black pepper
1½ cups buttermilk
3 tablespoons tomato paste
3 tablespoons oil
1 egg

This gorgeous golden bread with its heavenly aroma provides a lively accompaniment for soups, stews, or Italian food. Made without refined flours or hardened fats, it is healthful as well as delectable.

Sift together flour, baking powder, and soda, and stir in basil, thyme, and pepper. In separate bowl, whisk together buttermilk, tomato paste, oil, and egg until well blended. Add to dry ingredients and stir just until moistened. (Batter does not have to be smooth.) Spoon into buttered 9-inch loaf pan and bake in preheated 350°F oven for 45 to 55 minutes, or until top is crusty and deep golden, and center tests done.

Yield: One 9-inch loaf.

*Jennifer Stein
Canyon City, Oregon*

SQUASH SPOON BREAD

❧

1 cup milk
½ cup yellow or white cornmeal
1 cup cooked, mashed winter
　squash or pumpkin (or
　8 ounces canned)
1 tablespoon butter
½ teaspoon baking powder
¼ teaspoon salt
1 egg yolk, beaten
1 egg white, beaten stiff

Leftover squash or pumpkin works fine even if it was originally seasoned with brown sugar and spices. Serve this bread hot with butter, honey, or syrup.

Heat milk, stir in cornmeal, and cook 5 minutes, or until mixture thickens. Remove from heat and add squash, butter, baking powder, and salt, blending well. Let cool, then stir in beaten egg yolk, and fold in stiffly beaten egg white. Pour into greased 1-quart casserole and bake in preheated 375°F oven for 50 minutes, or until center tests done.

Yield: 4 to 6 servings.

*Ellen H. Gailey
Albuquerque, New Mexico*

CARROT CORN BREAD

❧

2 tablespoons plus 1 cup
  yellow cornmeal
¼ cup (½ stick) margarine,
  softened
2 tablespoons granulated sugar
⅓ cup light brown sugar
2 egg yolks
2 cups sifted cake flour
1 tablespoon baking powder
1 teaspoon salt
½ teaspoon baking soda
1 cup buttermilk
¾ cup cooked, mashed carrots
2 egg whites, stiffly beaten

A moist, colorful cornbread that does not crumble. It goes well with ham or hearty soups and makes a fine addition to brunch or a buffet table. Our recipe tester suggests using baby-food carrots if time is short and you don't have cooked carrots on hand. This corn bread can be frozen.

Grease 9-inch square baking pan, dust with 2 tablespoons of the cornmeal, shake off excess, and set aside. In large bowl, cream margarine and sugars until light and fluffy. Beat in egg yolks. Combine flour, remaining 1 cup cornmeal, baking powder, salt, and soda, and add to creamed mixture alternately with buttermilk, mixing just until moistened. Fold in carrots and then stiffly beaten egg whites. Spoon into prepared pan and bake in preheated 375°F oven for 25 to 30 minutes. Cut into squares and serve hot with butter.

Yield: 16 servings.

Constance M. Ellway
Hailey, Idaho

MEXICAN CORN BREAD

❧

2 eggs, beaten
⅔ cup oil
1 cup sour cream
1 cup creamed corn
1 cup yellow cornmeal
1 tablespoon baking powder
1½ teaspoons salt
  (or less to taste)
1 can (4 ounces) chopped
  green chilies, drained
1 cup grated sharp
  cheddar cheese

With our love for homemade Mexican food, this has become one of our favorite recipes (see page 55). The only complaint I get is that I don't fix it often enough.

Combine eggs, oil, sour cream, and creamed corn. In separate bowl, mix cornmeal, baking powder, and salt. Stir in egg mixture, chilies, and half the cheese. Spread into well-greased 9x13-inch pan and sprinkle with remaining cheese. Bake in preheated 425°F oven for 20 to 25 minutes.

Yield: 12 servings.

Peggy Hastings
Weatherford, Texas

YEAST BREADS

WHOLE-WHEAT BREAD

2 cups milk, scalded and
cooled (or water)
1 cup rolled oats
⅙ cup (3 to 3½ tablespoons)
cracked wheat
⅙ cup (3 to 3½ tablespoons)
wheat germ
⅙ cup (3 to 3½ tablespoons)
oat bran
½ cup sorghum or corn syrup
3 packages (3 tablespoons)
dry yeast
2 eggs (reserve 1 egg white)
2 teaspoons salt
½ cup (1 stick) butter, melted
1 cup dark rye flour
2 to 2½ cups whole-wheat flour
2 to 2½ cups unbleached
all-purpose flour
1 tablespoon water
2 teaspoons sesame seeds

An excellent stick-to-your-ribs bread that freezes well. Our recipe tester praised this as the best wheat bread she had ever tasted (see page 54).

In large bowl, combine milk, oats, cracked wheat, wheat germ, oat bran, sorghum, and yeast. Beat eggs, minus 1 egg white, and add to milk mixture. Stir in salt and cooled melted butter. Add flours alternately, 1 cup at a time, working in more flour, if needed, until dough can be easily handled.

Turn out onto floured surface and knead until smooth, about 10 minutes. Place dough in greased bowl, cover, and let rise until doubled in bulk.

Punch down, shape into 2 balls, and let rest 10 minutes. Shape into loaves, place in 2 well-greased 8½-inch loaf pans, and let rise until doubled.

Beat reserved egg white with 1 tablespoon water until frothy. Brush lightly over loaves, sprinkle with sesame seeds, and bake in preheated 350 to 375°F oven for 35 to 40 minutes. Remove from pans and cool on racks.

Yield: Two 8½-inch loaves.

Mrs. Arvin F. Brokaw
New Ross, Indiana

Multigrain Bread

2 packages (2 tablespoons)
    dry yeast
½ cup warm water
1 tablespoon salt
¼ cup oil
¼ cup honey
1½ cups warm potato water
    (saved from boiled potatoes)
2 cups warm water
1 cup rye flour
½ cup soy flour
½ cup wheat germ
½ cup wheat or oat bran
5 cups whole-wheat flour
3 cups unbleached
    stone-ground flour

I've tried several other bread recipes over the years but keep coming back to this one. It's simply better than any other, and my family likes it best, too. When I take it to potlucks and other get-togethers, it always receives compliments. To obtain the potato water, save the water drained from boiled potatoes and store it in the refrigerator until needed. It will keep for several weeks.

Dissolve yeast in ½ cup warm water and set aside for 5 minutes to proof. In large mixing bowl, combine salt, oil, honey, potato water, 2 cups warm water, and dissolved yeast mixture. Blend well. Add rye flour, soy flour, wheat germ, wheat bran, 2 cups of the whole-wheat flour, and 1 cup of the unbleached stone-ground flour, stirring until thoroughly incorporated. Set aside for 30 to 40 minutes to develop sponge (until mixture rises, is bubbly, and nearly fills bowl).

Stir in remaining 3 cups whole-wheat flour and 1 cup of the unbleached stone-ground flour. Turn out on floured surface and knead until smooth, using remaining cup of unbleached stone-ground flour. Place in greased bowl, turning once. Cover and let rise in warm place until doubled in bulk, about 1 hour.

Divide dough into three parts; knead each briefly and shape into loaf. Place in 3 greased 8½-inch loaf pans. Let rise until doubled, about 30 minutes. Place in cold oven, set temperature at 400°F, and bake for 10 minutes. Reduce to 350°F and bake 25 to 30 minutes. If bread darkens too rapidly while baking, cover lightly with foil.

Yield: Three 8½-inch loaves.

Alethea Thieszen
Bonner, Montana

CALIFORNIA SQUAW BREAD

❧

2 packages (2 tablespoons)
  dry yeast
1 teaspoon honey or
  granulated sugar
½ cup warm water
¼ cup molasses
½ cup raisins
¼ cup packed brown sugar
1¾ cups milk at room
  temperature, divided
⅓ cup butter or margarine, melted
1 tablespoon salt
1½ cups medium rye flour
2½ cups unbleached all-purpose
  or bread flour
2½ to 3 cups whole-wheat flour

Much better than the usual raisin bread, this is fantastic warm with butter, toasted, or used in a sandwich.

In large bowl of electric mixer, dissolve yeast and honey in water. Let stand 5 to 10 minutes, until foamy. Meanwhile, in blender or food processor fitted with metal blade, combine molasses, raisins, brown sugar, and ½ cup of the milk. Process 30 to 45 seconds, or until raisins are ground. Add to yeast mixture. Stir in remaining milk, cooled melted butter, salt, 1 cup of the rye flour, 1 cup of the all-purpose flour, and 1 cup of the whole-wheat flour. Beat at medium speed with electric mixer, or beat 200 vigorous strokes by hand. Stir in remaining rye and all-purpose flours, and enough remaining whole-wheat flour to make a soft dough.

Turn out onto floured board and knead 10 to 12 minutes, or until dough is smooth and elastic. Let rise in bowl covered with damp towel until doubled in bulk, about 1½ hours.

Punch down dough, let rest 10 minutes, and divide into 2 or 4 parts. Place in 2 greased 2-quart casserole dishes, two 9-inch loaf pans, or four 7-inch loaf pans, or shape into free-form loaves and place on greased baking sheet; set aside. Cover with dry towel and let rise again until doubled, about 1 hour.

Bake in preheated 375°F oven for 35 to 40 minutes for large loaves, or 25 to 30 minutes for small loaves, or until bread is nicely browned on top and has a hollow sound when tapped on bottom. Remove from pans, if using, and cool on racks.

Yield: 2 large or 4 small loaves.

Francine Derus
Westlake, Oregon

ITALIAN WHEAT BREAD

ᕷ

1 package (1 tablespoon)
  dry yeast
1 cup warm water
1 cup skim milk
1 teaspoon salt
¾ cup wheat bran
½ cup whole-wheat flour
1½ cups bread flour
2¾ cups unbleached
  all-purpose flour

This recipe is an original that I developed about a year ago. The bread has a great crust and is dense and chewy on the inside—characteristics of authentic Italian bread that one can find only in an "old world" bakery. High in fiber and low in fat, it can also be made without salt; however, to keep the taste from being too bland, I suggest adding herbs or other seasonings to the dough, such as ¼ cup fresh or 1 tablespoon dried basil, sage, or rosemary. It also is good lightly toasted and spread with a mixture of chopped tomatoes, basil, and olive oil. This bread freezes exceptionally well and can be defrosted and refrozen without loss of quality. Although I use a mixer and a dough hook, this equipment is not essential, nor are the wooden paddle and baking stone.

Soak yeast in ½ cup of the warm water for 10 minutes, or until it starts to bubble. Warm the skim milk and remaining ½ cup water. Add to yeast mixture along with salt, wheat bran, whole-wheat flour, and bread flour. Beat at medium speed of mixer for 2 minutes. Gradually add 1 cup of all-purpose flour and continue to beat for another 2 minutes. Attach dough hook to mixer. Gradually add remaining flour, using more if needed, until dough clings to hook. Knead for 8 to 10 minutes, adding more flour if dough sticks to sides of bowl.

Lightly oil large bowl with olive oil or nonstick cooking spray. Place dough in bowl and cover. Let rise in warm place for 1 hour, or until doubled in bulk.

Punch dough down. Sprinkle wooden paddle with cornmeal (if you don't have a paddle, you can use a heavy baking sheet) and turn on oven, with baking stone inside, to 400°F. (If you don't have a baking stone, do not preheat oven until 20 minutes before baking.)

Shape dough into tight, round loaf (almost evenly round like a ball, rather than flat and round) and place on paddle. Dust loaf with all-purpose flour and cover with dry kitchen towel. Let rise for 1 hour. (Do not overrise.)

(continued)

With a sharp bread knife, make 2 deep (¼- to ½-inch) slashes in top of loaf in crisscross pattern. Place loaf directly on baking stone and bake 50 to 55 minutes, or until crust is deep brown.

Yield: 1 round loaf.

Joanne Amato
Washington, D.C.

FAVORITE ALL-PURPOSE BREAD

ə

⅓ cup honey or molasses
3 cups warm water
1 package (1 tablespoon) dry yeast
3½ to 4 cups whole-wheat flour
3½ to 4 cups bread flour
1¼ tablespoons salt
½ cup oil
¾ cup chopped walnuts (optional)
¾ cup sunflower seeds

This recipe is special because it is so flexible. Sometimes I add wheat or oat bran, oats, and other high-fiber ingredients. Although the nuts are optional, they contribute to the flavor and texture. This makes a great sandwich bread, but it's equally good plain.

Dissolve honey in warm water, then stir in yeast. Add 2 cups of the whole-wheat flour and 2 cups of the bread flour, and mix well to make sponge. Set aside for about an hour.

Stir remaining flours, salt, oil, nuts (if using), and sunflower seeds into sponge. Knead about 10 minutes or process in food processor in batches. Set aside to rise.

Place in 2 greased and floured 8½-inch loaf pans, slash top lengthwise, and let rise another hour. Bake in preheated 350°F oven for 45 to 60 minutes.

Yield: Two 8½-inch loaves.

Susan Wynn
Woodstock, Georgia

WALNUT BREAD WITH ALLSPICE BUTTER

ॐ

2 packages (2 tablespoons)
  dry yeast (not quick-rising)
½ cup lukewarm water
1¾ cups skim milk, scalded
4 tablespoons butter or margarine
½ cup maple syrup or honey
1 tablespoon salt
7 to 8 cups flour
  (half whole-wheat and half
  unbleached all-purpose,
  or all whole-wheat)
1 cup coarsely chopped walnuts

ALLSPICE BUTTER
4 tablespoons butter or
  margarine, melted
½ teaspoon allspice

Nice, rich, dark loaves that are slightly sweet and have a fine, even texture.

Dissolve yeast in warm water. Pour scalded milk over butter, maple syrup, and salt, and stir to combine. Add 4 cups of the flour and softened yeast to form soft dough. Stir in nuts and remaining flour, and knead about 5 minutes. (Dough will be somewhat sticky.) Place dough in large oiled bowl, rotate to oil top, cover bowl, and let rise in warm place 1 to 1½ hours.

Punch down dough and shape into two loaves (loaves can be baked in 9-inch loaf pans or braided on baking sheets). Allow loaves to rise (covered) in warm place for 1 hour, or until doubled in bulk.

Bake loaves in preheated 350°F oven. After first 30 minutes, when bread forms crust, combine ingredients for the spiced butter and brush over tops. Bake loaves a total of about 1 hour, covering tops during baking if they become too brown. Brush loaves with remaining allspice butter after bread is baked but still warm.

Yield: Two 9-inch braided loaves.

Sally Gecks
Cincinnati, Ohio

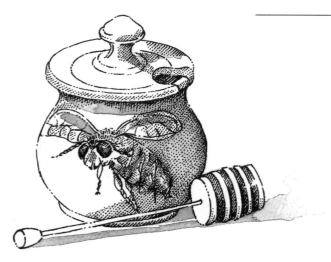

176

MIKE'S POTATO WHOLE-WHEAT BREAD

☙

2 large baking potatoes,
    washed and eyes removed
2 tablespoons salt
½ cup dark molasses
¼ cup olive oil (optional)
3 packages (3 tablespoons)
    dry yeast
10 to 12 cups whole-wheat flour

You'll never find this bread in a bakery. It is a fairly dense, chewy bread that's great for breakfast, sandwiches, and with chowders and stews. It's fun to make and looks great.

Cut unpeeled potatoes into pieces about 1x1x½-inch and boil until soft. Drain, but reserve the water, and mash until fairly smooth; you don't want large lumps in the bread.

Add enough water to the reserved potato water to make 4 cups and pour into large mixing bowl. Stir in salt, molasses, mashed potatoes, and olive oil (if using). Check temperature of mixture; it shouldn't be so hot that you can't leave your finger in it. Stir in yeast and 4 cups of the flour, or enough to make a thick, barely stirrable batter. Beat 100 strokes with a wooden spoon, scraping the sides of the bowl frequently. Cover and let dough rise until doubled.

Stir in more flour and begin kneading. (If your bowl is big enough, you can knead right in it and save some cleanup time.) After 15 minutes or so, dough should be elastic yet slightly sticky, not too dry. Cover and let rise until doubled.

Punch dough down and divide into 3 equal pieces. Shape each into a loaf and place in 3 greased 8½-inch loaf pans. Make a slash in each loaf and let rise until doubled.

Bake in preheated 375°F oven for 50 to 60 minutes; remove a loaf after 50 minutes and thump the bottom. If it sounds hollow, knife-test the loaf to make sure that it's baked through. If it doesn't test done, bake for another 10 minutes.

Yield: Three 8½-inch loaves.

Michael J. Russell
Norfolk, Virginia

BEAN & BUTTER BREAD

ઠ

1 can (15 ounces) kidney beans, undrained
⅓ cup molasses
⅓ cup peanut butter
⅓ cup oil
1 egg, beaten
3 tablespoons sugar
1 teaspoon salt
1 cup hot water (120 to 130°F)
3 packages (3 tablespoons) dry yeast
5½ to 6 cups unbleached all-purpose flour
1 cup whole-wheat flour
1 egg white
2 tablespoons water

My sister gave me this recipe. The beans add extra fiber and an unusual texture, and the peanut butter gives a unique flavor. The bread makes great sandwiches, goes well with soups and stews, and also works for party canapés. Cut into shapes and spread with liver pâté, or serve with any good yogurt or sour cream dip.

Place kidney beans, molasses, peanut butter, oil, egg, sugar, and salt in blender or food processor container and blend until smooth. Pour into large mixing bowl and stir in hot water. Combine yeast with 4 cups of the all-purpose flour, add to bean mixture, and blend well. Stir in whole-wheat flour. Work in remaining all-purpose flour in gradual amounts to form a stiff dough.

Knead until smooth and elastic. Shape into ball and place in greased bowl. Cover loosely and let stand at room temperature until doubled in size, about 1½ hours.

Punch dough down, cover loosely, and let rest 15 minutes. Shape into 2 round loaves and place on greased baking sheet. Combine egg white with 2 tablespoons water and brush on tops of loaves. With sharp knife, cut diagonal slashes ⅛ inch deep and about 2½ inches apart across top of loaves. Bake in preheated 350°F oven for 55 minutes, or until done.

Yield: Two 8-inch round loaves.

Christina K. Richter
Minot, North Dakota

WHOLE-WHEAT & OATMEAL BREAD

ð

2 cups boiling water
1 cup rolled oats
1 tablespoon safflower oil
1 package (1 tablespoon) dry yeast
½ cup warm water
1½ teaspoons salt
⅙ cup molasses
⅙ cup honey
1 cup whole-wheat flour
3 to 4 cups unbleached all-purpose flour
⅜ cup noninstant dried milk (optional)

A variation of this recipe was given to me in 1963 by Helen Philbrick. Helen was a wonderful bread baker, and when I was just starting out, she gave me many helpful tips. I altered the original recipe by adding whole-wheat flour, changing butter to safflower oil, and adding honey. This nicely textured bread is excellent toasted and firm enough to slice for sandwiches.

In large bowl, pour boiling water over oats and oil, stir to blend, and let sit 1 hour.

Combine yeast and warm water and set aside to soften. Add to oats mixture along with salt, molasses, honey, flours, and dried milk powder (if using), and blend well. Knead until smooth and elastic, and let rise until doubled.

Place in 2 well-greased 8½-inch loaf pans, let rise until dough is above rims of pans, and bake in preheated 350°F oven for about 45 minutes.

Yield: Two 8½-inch loaves.

Diane Hutchins Anderson
Bloomington, Minnesota

OATMEAL BREAD

෧

2 cups boiling water
1 cup rolled oats
1 tablespoon butter
½ cup molasses
2 teaspoons salt
½ cup lukewarm water
1 package (1 tablespoon)
  dry yeast
7 to 7½ cups unbleached
  all-purpose flour

My dear friend and fellow worker Doris Levanitis gave me this recipe. It is low in fat yet will stay moist for several days. The loaves are nicely rounded and compact with a slightly sweet, molasses flavor and a dense, fine grain.

Combine boiling water, rolled oats, and butter in large mixing bowl. Stir thoroughly and let stand 1 hour. Stir in molasses and salt. In small bowl, mix lukewarm water and yeast. When dissolved, add to oats mixture. Stir in 4½ cups flour and beat thoroughly. Cover and let rise until doubled in bulk.

Add enough additional flour (several cups) to make dough just firm enough to handle. Knead until smooth and elastic, then cover and let rest 10 to 15 minutes.

Shape into loaves and place in 2 buttered 9-inch loaf pans. Let rise until almost doubled in bulk (about 1 hour at room temperature). Bake in preheated 350°F oven for 35 to 45 minutes, or until bread tests done.

Yield: Two 9-inch loaves.

Patricia DeLoughrey
North Easton, Massachusetts

NUTRITIOUS DOUBLE-OAT BREAD

¾ cup steel-cut oats
½ cup rolled oats
¼ cup honey
1 tablespoon canola oil
2 cups boiling water
1 package quick-rising yeast
1 teaspoon sugar
¼ cup warm water
3 egg whites (reserve
  1 tablespoon for glaze)
½ cup skim milk powder
¼ cup sunflower seeds (optional)
1 cup whole-wheat flour
3 to 4 cups unbleached
  all-purpose flour (approximately)

The deep golden crust and flecks of oats give this the look of a hearty peasant bread. Sunflower seeds add a nutty quality and texture, as well as visual appeal. Although low in fat and cholesterol and without salt, this bread is moist, flavorful, and a good keeper.

Combine oats, honey, oil, and 2 cups boiling water in large bowl, mix, and let cool. In separate bowl, mix yeast, sugar, and ¼ cup warm water, and stir into cooled oats mixture. Add egg whites except for reserved 1 tablespoon, milk powder, sunflower seeds (if using), whole-wheat flour, and 1 cup all-purpose flour, blending well. Let rest for 45 minutes.

Turn out onto floured surface and knead for 15 minutes, adding more flour as needed for dough to form a ball. It should be a little sticky, not dry. Place in oiled bowl and cover. Let rise until doubled, about 1 hour.

Punch down dough, shape into loaf or loaves, and place in 1 greased 9-inch loaf pan or 2 greased 7-inch loaf pans. Cover with towel and let rise until doubled. Brush with reserved egg white and bake in preheated 325°F oven for 30 to 45 minutes, or until brown and sounds hollow when tapped. Turn out on rack to cool.

Yield: One 9-inch or two 7-inch loaves.

Melitta White
Eagle River, Arkansas

BUCKWHEAT BREAD

2

2 packages (2 tablespoons)
  dry yeast
1½ cups warm water
1 cup undiluted evaporated milk
½ cup molasses
2½ teaspoons salt
2 tablespoons oil
1 cup buckwheat flour
½ cup raisins
3 cups unbleached
  all-purpose flour

I don't cut these beautiful loaves of braided bread, but encourage my company to tear off pieces. Although the quantity of molasses called for may sound like a lot, it is just the right amount to balance the somewhat bitter taste of buckwheat flour.

In large bowl, make sponge by combining yeast, warm water, evaporated milk, molasses, salt, oil, buckwheat flour, and raisins. Set aside until foamy, an hour or so.

Stir in all-purpose flour until dough is stiff, then knead until smooth and elastic. Place in oiled bowl and let rise until doubled.

Punch dough down, divide in two, then divide each half into thirds. Roll each third into a rope 16 to 18 inches long, then pinch the ends together and braid. Coil both braids into 9-inch-diameter unglazed-pottery flowerpot saucers that have been greased (or use greased 9-inch Pyrex pie pans), and let rise until doubled. Place in cold oven, set temperature to 350°F, and bake for 40 minutes.

Yield: Two 9-inch round loaves.

Diane TenEyck
Cottage Grove, Oregon

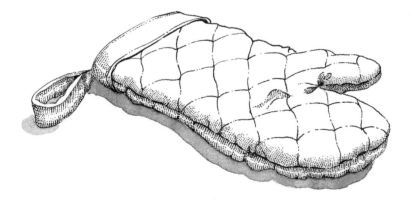

182

RAISIN BREAD

ð

3½ cups unbleached
  all-purpose flour
2 tablespoons sugar
1 package quick-rising yeast
½ teaspoon salt
2 tablespoons butter, melted
1⅓ cups hot water (125 to 130°F)
½ to ¾ cup raisins
¼ cup sugar
1 teaspoon cinnamon

Swirled with cinnamon-sugar and dotted with raisins, this appealing bread is easy enough to make frequently for the family and fancy enough to serve to company.

Mix flour, 2 tablespoons sugar, yeast, and salt in bowl. Stir in butter and water, making very thick batter. Add raisins and blend in well. Cover and let rise until doubled in bulk, about 30 minutes. Combine ¼ cup sugar and cinnamon, and set aside.

Stir down dough and turn out onto floured surface. Flatten dough, pour sugar-cinnamon mixture in stripes across surface, and fold dough into loaf shape. Place in greased 9-inch loaf pan and tuck any raisins poking through dough back inside so they don't burn while baking. Cover and let rise until doubled.

Bake in preheated 375°F oven for 35 minutes or until done. Remove from pan and cool on rack.

Yield: One 9-inch loaf.

Victor Degni
Vernon, New York

APPLE-RAISIN BREAD BRAID

ɞ

½ cup warm milk (105 to 115°F)
1 package (1 tablespoon)
   dry yeast
¼ cup sugar
1 large egg at room temperature
¼ cup (½ stick) butter
   at room temperature
½ teaspoon salt
2½ to 2¾ cups unbleached
   all-purpose flour

FILLING
4 cups peeled, cored, and
   chopped apples
¾ cup raisins
¼ cup firmly packed
   brown sugar
½ teaspoon cinnamon

Although time-consuming, this recipe actually is quite simple once you've made it a couple of times. When cutting the sides of the dough into strips, be sure not to make them too long or the filling will leak out during baking.

In large bowl, combine milk, yeast, and sugar; let stand 2 minutes. Add egg, butter, salt, and 1¼ cups of the flour. Mix until smooth, then beat 2 minutes. Stir in enough remaining flour to make soft dough. Turn out onto well-floured surface and knead 6 to 8 minutes until smooth and elastic, adding only as much flour as needed to prevent dough from sticking. Place in greased bowl and rotate to grease top. Cover with damp towel and let rise in warm place until doubled, about 1½ hours.

While dough is rising, prepare filling to ensure that it is cold before using in braid. In medium-size saucepan, combine apples, raisins, brown sugar, and cinnamon, and cook over medium heat until fruit is soft and pulpy, about 10 minutes. Remove from heat and cool in refrigerator.

After dough has risen, punch it down and turn out onto lightly floured surface. Roll out into 8x14-inch rectangle. Spread fruit filling lengthwise down center, covering a space about 3 inches wide. On each side of filling, make cuts 2 inches long at 1-inch intervals. Take strips from each side and cross them over filling to form braid. Tuck last 2 strips underneath. Transfer to baking sheet, cover, and let rise in warm place until doubled in bulk, about 30 minutes.

Bake in preheated 350°F oven until top is light brown, about 20 to 25 minutes. Cover with foil during last 10 minutes to prevent overbrowning.

Yield: 1 braided loaf.

Valerie Jordan
Fife Lake, Michigan

APRICOT-PECAN BREAD

❧

2 packages (2 tablespoons)
  dry yeast
4 to 5 cups unbleached
  all-purpose flour
⅓ cup sugar
2 teaspoons salt
½ rounded teaspoon ginger
½ rounded teaspoon nutmeg
¼ cup (½ stick) margarine
1½ cups skim milk
1 egg
¾ cup chopped dried apricots
¾ cup finely chopped pecans
Softened margarine
Sugar

Healthful and delicious, this is marvelous for breakfast or teatime. I began making it after my husband had a heart bypass operation and we all became much more conscious of the need for low-cholesterol foods. Sugar-free apricot preserves, spread on each slice, bring out the flavor.

Combine yeast, 4 cups of the flour, ⅓ cup sugar, salt, ginger, and nutmeg in large mixer bowl. Heat ¼ cup margarine in skim milk until warm (120 to 130°F); it does not need to melt completely. Blend into flour mixture, then add egg. Beat at low speed until moist, then at medium speed for 3 minutes. By hand, stir in apricots and pecans, and, if needed, add more flour to make a firm dough.

Turn out onto well-floured surface and knead for about 8 minutes, or until smooth and elastic. Place in greased bowl, cover with dish towel, and let rise until doubled.

Punch dough down and divide into 2 equal parts. Roll each half into a 7x14-inch rectangle. Starting from short (7-inch) side, roll up dough tightly and pinch ends to seal. Place rolls in greased and floured 8-inch loaf pans. Cover again and let rise until doubled.

Bake in preheated 375°F oven for 25 to 30 minutes, or until golden in color. Remove from oven, brush with softened margarine, and sprinkle with sugar.

Yield: Two 8-inch loaves.

Elizabeth Léonie Simpson
Woodside, California

MOUNTAINEER MAPLE BREAD

❧

4½ to 5½ cups unbleached
  all-purpose flour
2 packages (2 tablespoons)
  dry yeast
¾ cup maple syrup
½ cup milk
½ cup water
½ cup oil
2 teaspoons salt
1 egg
1 egg yolk
1 egg white, slightly beaten
1 tablespoon water

My husband, Roger (the mountaineer), has been making this bread for 23 years, and it has become a staple at our Thanksgiving table. It can be braided or shaped other ways, too, and makes fabulous toast the next day if there's any left!

Spoon flour into dry measuring cup and level. Do not scoop. Sift together 2 cups flour and yeast. Heat maple syrup, milk, ½ cup water, oil, and salt over low heat only until warm, stirring to blend. Add to flour-yeast mixture and beat until smooth, about 2 minutes on medium speed of electric mixer or 300 strokes by hand. Blend in whole egg and yolk. Add 1 more cup of the flour and beat 1 minute on medium speed or 150 strokes by hand. Stir in more flour to make a moderately stiff dough. Turn out onto lightly floured surface and knead until smooth and satiny, 8 to 10 minutes. Shape into ball and place in lightly greased bowl, turning to grease all sides. Cover and let rise until doubled.

Punch down dough, divide into fourths, cover, and let rest 10 minutes. Shape 3 of the 4 portions into balls. Place on greased baking sheet, in cloverleaf design, and flatten each to 1-inch thickness. Cut remaining dough into quarters. With palms of hands, roll each quarter into 20-inch rope. Entwine two of the ropes, forming a kind of braid, and press ends to seal. Repeat with remaining 2 ropes. Arrange on top of cloverleaf to form a "crown" of sorts, tucking the ends under. Cover and let rise until doubled.

Combine egg white and 1 tablespoon water, and brush on loaf. Bake in preheated 350°F oven for 40 to 50 minutes, or until done. If necessary, cover loosely with foil to prevent overbrowning. Remove from baking sheet immediately and let cool on rack.

Yield: 1 large loaf.

Alison Hull
Cedar Crest, New Mexico

EAGLES BREAD

❧

2¼ cups buttermilk
2 tablespoons clover honey
½ stick butter or margarine
5½ to 6½ cups bread flour
1 package quick-rising yeast
½ teaspoon salt

I make this bread every week, with my "Eagles Greatest Hits: Volume I" tape playing. I'm not exactly sure if the music contributes to the final product, but it certainly makes bread baking a lot more fun! Great for sandwiches, this also is fantastic as French toast.

In small saucepan, combine buttermilk, honey, and butter, and heat to 120 to 125°F. Place 3 cups of the flour in large bowl, stir in yeast and salt, and beat in warm buttermilk mixture. Beat for about 5 minutes. By hand, stir in about 2½ cups more flour, mixing until dough leaves sides of bowl.

Turn out dough onto floured surface and knead 10 to 12 minutes, adding flour as needed to prevent sticking. When smooth and elastic, place in greased bowl and rotate to grease all surfaces. Cover and let rise in warm place until doubled, about 45 minutes.

Punch down dough, divide in half, form 2 loaves, and place in 2 greased 9-inch loaf pans. Cover and let rise until doubled, about 45 minutes.

Bake in preheated 425°F oven for 10 minutes, lower heat to 350°F, and bake another 25 to 30 minutes. Remove from pans immediately and cool on rack.

Yield: Two 9-inch loaves.

Shermy Bremer
Irons, Michigan

PEDA BREAD

❧

2 packages (2 tablespoons)
  dry yeast
2 cups warm water (about 110°F)
2 tablespoons sugar
1 tablespoon salt
3 tablespoons butter or
  margarine, melted
5½ to 6 cups unbleached
  all-purpose flour
2 teaspoons toasted sesame seeds
  or poppy seeds (optional)

FLOUR GLAZE
2 teaspoons unbleached
  all-purpose flour
½ cup cold water

Suited to any occasion or time of day, this interestingly shaped bread has a shiny, crunchy crust, light flavor, and chewy texture. (See page 136.)

In large bowl, dissolve yeast in water. Stir in sugar, salt, and melted butter. Gradually beat in about 5 cups of the flour to make a stiff dough.

Turn out onto floured board and knead until smooth, adding flour as needed to prevent sticking. Place dough in greased bowl and rotate so all surfaces are greased; cover and let rise in warm place until doubled, about 1 hour.

Lightly grease 2 large baking sheets and dust with flour. Punch down dough, divide into 2 equal parts, and shape each into smooth ball. Set both balls on baking sheets, cover lightly, and let rest at room temperature for 30 minutes. Then press, pull, and pound with your fist to shape each loaf into an oval about 11x14 inches. Cover and let rise in warm place until doubled, 45 to 60 minutes.

Using soft brush dipped in cool water, brush top and sides of each loaf. Then dip fingertips in water, and with the 4 fingertips of each hand lined up, mark bread like this: Press down to baking sheet, marking first a 1½-inch-wide border around edge, then lines crosswise and lengthwise, about 2 inches apart. Let rise, uncovered, until almost doubled, about 45 minutes.

Meanwhile, prepare the glaze. In small saucepan, blend flour with water until smooth. Place over medium heat and cook, stirring, until mixture boils and thickens. Remove from heat and let stand, covered, until ready to use.

Bake bread, one loaf at a time, in center of preheated 450°F oven for about 15 minutes, or until golden brown. As each loaf comes from oven, lightly apply flour glaze with soft brush over sides and top.

(continued)

If you wish to add seeds, brush each loaf again lightly with glaze and sprinkle with seeds. Cool on racks.

Yield: Two 11x14-inch loaves, 10 to 12 servings each.

Debbie Roberts
Lake City, Minnesota

OLD-ORDER AMISH BREAD

2a

1 package (1 tablespoon) dry yeast
1½ cups warm water (115 to 120°F)
5 to 6 cups bread flour
2 tablespoons sugar
2 teaspoons salt
⅓ cup canola oil

I make this every week. It is a moist, attractively shaped, no-nonsense white bread and has a nice brown crust.

Stir yeast into water and set aside for 5 minutes. In large bowl, combine 2 cups of the flour, sugar, salt, and oil. Add yeast to flour mixture and blend well. Add remaining flour, ½ cup at a time, until dough leaves sides of bowl. (Dough should be elastic, not sticky.)

Turn out onto floured surface and knead 8 minutes. Place in greased bowl and rotate to grease top. Cover with plastic wrap and let rise until doubled, about 1 hour.

Punch down dough, re-cover, and let rise again, for 45 minutes. Punch down and knead again. Divide into 2 pieces, shape into loaves, and place in 2 greased 8½-inch loaf pans. Cover and let rise again until dough is 1 inch above pan rims, about 40 minutes.

Bake in preheated 400°F oven for 10 minutes. Reduce heat to 350°F and bake 25 to 30 minutes. Remove from pans and cool.

Yield: Two 8½-inch loaves.

Freda Nolan
Warren, Michigan

GRAHAM-FLOUR BREAD

❧

4 to 6 cups unbleached
  all-purpose flour
  (preferably Better for Bread)
2 cups graham flour
3 tablespoons wheat gluten
3 teaspoons instant active
  dry yeast
½ stick margarine, melted
2¾ cups buttermilk
1 teaspoon salt
1 teaspoon baking soda
½ cup brown sugar
1 egg, beaten

In 1942, after I had finished medical school, my internship, and four years as a postgraduate surgical resident, my wife and I took the first vacation we had had in over nine years. We went to a remote fishing resort on Face Lake, north of Kamloops, British Columbia. It was so isolated we had to pack in on horseback for 12 miles. This is where I had my first taste of real, old-fashioned homemade bread. It was so delicious that I obtained a copy of the recipe, but in our subsequent moving around, the recipe was misplaced for over 40 years, when I found it tucked away in a drawer. The bread originally had been made in an old farmhouse kitchen with a wood range, so I had to adjust the recipe to our modern electric range. I use Better for Bread flour because the higher protein gives more gluten, which makes a strong network to support the risen dough. I also add a bit of wheat gluten for additional support.

Combine 4 cups of the all-purpose flour, the graham flour, wheat gluten, and yeast. In separate bowl, mix together cooled melted margarine, buttermilk, salt, soda, brown sugar, and egg. Stir into flour mixture and beat well. Add additional all-purpose flour as needed to make a firm dough. Let rise in greased bowl for 45 minutes to 1 hour.

Divide dough into 2 equal portions. Knead into small rounds, and let rest for about 10 minutes. Transfer to 2 greased 9-inch loaf pans and let rise in warm place for about 20 to 25 minutes, just until bread is at tops of pans. Bake in preheated 375°F oven for 10 minutes, reduce heat to 350°F, and bake for another 25 to 30 minutes, or until bread tests done. Cool on racks.

Yield: Two 9-inch loaves.

Richard H. Humphreys
Spokane, Washington

HIGH-PROTEIN HONEY WHEAT BREAD

৯

4 cups unbleached
   all-purpose flour
2 teaspoons salt
2 packages (2 tablespoons)
   dry yeast
1 cup water
½ cup honey
¼ cup (½ stick) margarine
1 small carton (8 ounces)
   small-curd cottage cheese
2 eggs
2 cups whole-wheat flour
½ cup rolled oats
   (quick-cooking oats okay)
1 cup chopped nuts
Shortening

This tasty, nutritious bread is lighter than one would think. The dough is somewhat stiff, so kneading requires a bit of elbow grease, but you won't regret the time and effort.

In large mixing bowl, combine 2 cups of the all-purpose flour, salt, and yeast, stirring well. In medium saucepan, heat water, honey, margarine, and cottage cheese until very warm but not hot. Stir into flour mixture. Add eggs and blend at low speed until moistened, then beat 3 minutes at medium speed. Stir in whole-wheat flour, oats, and nuts, plus 2 more cups of all-purpose flour to form a soft dough.

Turn out onto floured surface and cover with bowl. Let rest for 10 to 15 minutes, then knead for 5 minutes until smooth and elastic. Place in greased bowl, cover with towel, and let rise in warm place until doubled (1 to 1½ hours).

Divide in 2 pieces and shape into loaves. Place in greased 8-inch loaf pans, pierce tops with fork in 4 or 5 places, and let rise until doubled (45 to 60 minutes). Bake in preheated 350°F oven for 30 to 40 minutes. Brush tops lightly with shortening to keep crusts soft.

Yield: Two 8-inch loaves.

Nancy Harrison
Royal Oaks, Maryland

CINDY'S WHEATBERRY BREAD

ʕ

1 tablespoon sugar
½ cup warm water
1 package (1 tablespoon)
   dry yeast
4 eggs
⅓ cup oil
½ cup sugar
2½ cups warm water
1 teaspoon salt
3 tablespoons lemon juice
1 to 2 cups cooked wheatberries
   (see Note next page)
4 to 5 cups unbleached
   all-purpose flour
5 to 6 cups whole-wheat flour
1 egg, beaten lightly (optional)
2 tablespoons sesame seeds
   (optional)

This is a slightly sweet, very nutritious bread with a pleasing aroma and lovely appearance. I buy hard winter wheat in 50-pound bags and grind my own flour. This recipe is versatile in that honey or molasses can be used instead of sugar, and cooked oatmeal or bulgur soaked in boiling water for 1 hour can replace the wheatberries.

Mix 1 tablespoon sugar and ½ cup warm water in small bowl and sprinkle yeast on top. Let sit about 10 minutes, or until it proofs or "blooms." In very large (8- to 12-quart) mixing bowl, lightly beat eggs with fork. Add oil, ½ cup sugar, 2½ cups warm water, salt, lemon juice, wheatberries, and yeast mixture; stir well. With wooden spoon, gradually stir in about 4 cups of the all-purpose flour and 4 to 5 cups of the whole-wheat flour. Continue to stir and add flours as needed until dough gets somewhat stiff.

Turn out onto floured surface and knead until smooth and elastic, adding more flour as needed. Let bread rest while you wash out mixing bowl and dry and oil it. Place dough in bowl, turn to oil top, and cover with wax paper. Let rise in warm place until doubled (about 1 hour).

Punch dough down and cut in half. Divide one half into 2 equal amounts and place in 2 greased 8½-inch loaf pans. Set in warm place to rise until doubled (about 1 hour).

Cut remaining half of dough into 8 to 12 equal pieces. Pat out into round, flat (¾-inch-high) shapes, a little bigger around than hamburger buns. Place on greased baking sheets and set in warm place to rise for about 30 minutes.

If desired, brush tops of rolls with beaten egg for glossy brown finish and sprinkle with sesame seeds. Bake in preheated 375°F oven for 18 to 20 minutes, or until nicely browned and rolls sound slightly hollow when tapped.

When loaves have doubled in bulk, slash tops, and if desired, brush with egg wash and sprinkle with sesame seeds. Bake

(continued)

at 375°F for 40 to 45 minutes, or until nicely browned and loaves sound hollow when tapped. Remove from pans and cool on rack.

Note: Four hours ahead of time or the day before, combine 1 cup wheatberries with 4 cups water. Bring to boil and simmer, covered, for about 4 hours, or simmer for 2 hours, turn off heat, and leave covered overnight. In the morning, simmer again for 1 hour, or until berries are tender.

Yield: 8 to 12 rolls and two 8½-inch loaves.

Cindy Tompkins
Creswell, Oregon

MASSACHUSETTS ANADAMA BREAD

❧

2 cups water
½ cup yellow cornmeal
2 tablespoons butter
½ cup molasses
2 tablespoons salt
2 packages (2 tablespoons) dry yeast
½ cup warm water
7½ cups unbleached all-purpose flour

This is a hearty, plate-mopping bread. I got the recipe from a farmer in West Newbury, Massachusetts, where it was traditionally served each Saturday night with ham and baked beans.

In saucepan, combine 2 cups water, cornmeal, butter, molasses, and salt. Stir over low heat until mixture bubbles and thickens slightly. Cool to lukewarm.

Pour yeast into large bowl and stir in ½ cup warm water (105°F). Add cornmeal mixture and gradually stir in flour until stiff dough is formed.

Turn out onto heavily floured surface and knead 5 minutes, or until dough is smooth and elastic (it should hold together well). Place in greased bowl, cover, and let rise until doubled in bulk (about 1 hour).

Punch down and knead again a few times. Cut dough with sharp knife into 2 equal parts and pat both into 9-inch squares. Roll each square tightly like a jelly roll and place seam side down in greased 9-inch loaf pan. Let rise for 45 minutes.

Bake in preheated 350°F oven for 40 to 45 minutes, or until golden brown. Do not overbake. When done, loaf will have dull hollow sound when thumped on bottom.

Yield: Two 9-inch loaves.

*Terry Thompson
Somersworth, New Hampshire*

SUNDIAL FARM ANADAMA BREAD

&

1 cup rolled oats
  (organic preferred)
1 cup cornmeal
  (organic preferred)
2 teaspoons salt
2 cups boiling water
1 stick margarine, melted
½ cup molasses
1 cup warm water
2 packages (2 tablespoons)
  dry yeast
1 cup whole-wheat flour
4½ to 5 cups unbleached
  all-purpose flour

This is a delectable, moist, and easy bread. Sometimes I use part of the dough for homemade pizza. My husband, Paul Dumanoski, says, "Anadama good bread it is!"

Measure oats and cornmeal into very large bowl and add salt. Pour in 2 cups boiling water and melted margarine, stirring to moisten completely. Pour molasses into 2-cup liquid measuring cup, then pour into hot mixture, blending well. Let mixture cool to lukewarm (15 to 20 minutes).

When mixture is almost lukewarm, pour 1 cup warm water into measuring cup that held molasses and slowly stir in yeast to dissolve. (The yeast will become activated and feed on what little molasses there is left in the cup.)

When yeast mixture is foamy, stir into oats, mixing well, then add whole-wheat and 4 cups of the all-purpose flour. (Mixture will be moist.) Cover and let rise in warm place until doubled (about 1 hour).

Sprinkle additional ½ to 1 cup all-purpose flour over top, stir in, and turn out onto floured surface. Knead 10 minutes. Divide in half and place in 2 greased 7-inch loaf pans. Let rise, covered, until doubled. Bake in preheated 350°F oven for 35 minutes.

Yield: Two 7-inch loaves.

Mary Ellen Radziewicz
Barre, Massachusetts

EARLY COLONIAL BREAD

ба

½ cup yellow cornmeal
½ cup brown sugar
1 tablespoon salt
2 cups boiling water
¼ cup oil
2 packages (2 tablespoons)
  dry yeast
½ cup lukewarm water
¾ cup whole-wheat flour
½ cup rye flour
4¼ to 4½ cups sifted bread flour
  (or unbleached all-purpose)

I am 61 years old and have baked bread for many years. I use this recipe often but don't remember where I got it. We like it sliced thick and toasted.

Combine cornmeal, brown sugar, and salt in large bowl. Gradually pour in 2 cups boiling water, stirring continuously to prevent lumps. Blend in oil and set aside to cool to lukewarm, at least 30 minutes.

Soften yeast in ½ cup lukewarm water. Stir into cooled cornmeal mixture, then add whole-wheat and rye flours, mixing well. Add enough bread flour to make moderately stiff dough.

Turn out onto lightly floured surface and knead until smooth and elastic, about 6 to 8 minutes. Place in greased bowl, turn over to grease top, cover, and let rise in warm place until doubled (50 to 60 minutes).

Punch down dough and turn out onto lightly floured surface. Divide in half, cover, and let rest for 10 minutes. Shape into 2 loaves and place in greased 9-inch loaf pans. Let rise until doubled.

Bake in preheated 350°F oven for 45 minutes, or until bread tests done. Cap loosely with foil after first 25 minutes if browning too rapidly.

Yield: Two 9-inch loaves.

Norma Meddaugh
West Allis, Wisconsin

HEALTH BREAD

2 packages (2 tablespoons)
   dry yeast
¼ cup warm water
½ cup warm milk (110 to 115°F)
5 to 6 cups bread flour
   (or unbleached all-purpose)
1 cup whole-wheat flour
1 cup rye flour
½ cup honey
½ cup molasses
¼ cup (½ stick) margarine
1 tablespoon salt
1½ cups hot water
2 eggs

Sweet, hearty, and satisfying, this is a fantastic anytime-of-day, every-day bread. The extra step of making a sponge adds appreciably to the flavor and texture.

Make sponge by mixing yeast in warm water to soften. Stir in warm milk and ¾ cup of the bread flour. Set aside in warm place until bubbly and almost doubled in size (about 15 minutes).

Meanwhile, mix together whole-wheat flour, rye flour, honey, molasses, margarine, salt, and hot water. Stir until well blended and cool to lukewarm. Add eggs and beat thoroughly. Mix the two doughs together and stir in 4½ cups of the bread flour. Turn out onto floured surface and knead for 10 to 15 minutes, using additional flour if needed, until bread is smooth and elastic. Let rise until doubled in bulk.

Punch down dough, shape into 3 loaves, and place in greased 9-inch loaf pans. Let rise again, then bake in preheated 350°F oven for 30 to 45 minutes.

Yield: Three 9-inch loaves.

Diana Stapley
Grand Rapids, Michigan

EVERYONE'S FAVORITE BRAIDED BREAD

⁊

4½ cups unbleached
   all-purpose flour
2 tablespoons sugar
1 tablespoon salt
2 packages (2 tablespoons)
   dry yeast
¼ cup (½ stick) margarine,
   softened
2¼ cups very warm water
   (120 to 130°F)
4 tablespoons molasses, divided
1¼ cups whole-wheat flour
1 teaspoon caraway seeds
1 tablespoon cocoa
1½ cups rye flour

This looks impressive with the three colors of bread braided together. The flavor of each braid is distinctive, yet blends well with the others. Ideal for a fancy meal or brunch buffet.

In large bowl, combine 2¼ cups of the all-purpose flour, sugar, salt, and yeast. Add margarine and warm water, and beat 2 minutes on medium speed. Add another cup of all-purpose flour and beat 2 additional minutes.

Divide batter among 3 bowls. In first bowl, beat in 2 tablespoons molasses and whole-wheat flour. In second bowl, beat in 2 tablespoons molasses, caraway seeds, cocoa, and rye flour. In third bowl, beat in 1¼ cups all-purpose flour.

Knead each portion until smooth and elastic (about 5 minutes). Cover and let rise in warm place until doubled in size (about 1 hour).

Starting with one of the 3 bowls, punch down dough and turn out onto floured surface. Divide in half and roll both halves into 15-inch ropes. Repeat with dough in other 2 bowls, creating a total of 6 ropes of 3 kinds of dough. Place 3 ropes (one of each kind of bread dough) on greased baking sheet and braid together. Pinch ends and fold under to seal. Repeat with remaining 3 ropes. Cover and let rise until doubled.

Bake in preheated 350°F oven for 30 to 40 minutes, or until tests done. Cool on rack.

Yield: 2 braided loaves.

Liz Wehrmacher
Waverly, Iowa

RUSSIAN BLACK BREAD

ᴥ

4 cups rye flour
3 cups unbleached
  all-purpose flour
1 teaspoon sugar
2 teaspoons salt
2 cups All-Bran cereal
2 tablespoons caraway seeds
2 teaspoons crushed fennel seeds
2 packages (2 tablespoons)
  dry yeast
2½ cups water
¼ cup white vinegar
⅓ cup unsulfured molasses
¼ cup (½ stick) butter
2 teaspoons instant coffee powder
1 square (1 ounce) unsweetened
  chocolate

This is not how our Russian friends make black bread, but it works for me. The loaves are dense and dark, with a rich, slightly tangy, complex flavor. Excellent with soups.

Mix rye and all-purpose flours together. In large bowl, combine 2½ cups of flour mixture with sugar, salt, cereal, caraway seeds, fennel seeds, and yeast. In saucepan, combine water, vinegar, molasses, butter, coffee powder, and chocolate. Heat until very warm, but do not boil. Gradually add to flour-yeast mixture, and beat 2 minutes with mixer at medium speed. Add ½ cup more of flour mixture and beat on high speed for 2 minutes.

Stir in 2½ more cups of flour mixture and turn out onto floured surface. Knead for 15 minutes, working in remaining flour. Place in greased bowl, cover, and let rise until doubled.

Punch down dough, divide in half, and shape into 2 balls. Place in 2 greased 8-inch round pans. Cover and let rise until doubled. Bake in preheated 350°F oven for 45 minutes.

Yield: Two 8-inch round loaves.

Kristin E. Glick-Nuckolls
Elgin, Illinois

GROSSMUTTER'S RYE-MEAL BREAD

ဆ

2 packages (2 tablespoons)
    dry yeast
4½ cups warm water
⅓ cup shortening, melted
2 tablespoons salt
⅔ cup molasses
3 cups rye meal
8 cups unbleached
    all-purpose flour
    (or more as needed)

This recipe was handed down by my great-grandmother, who came to this country from Germany. The bread is hearty without having an overwhelmingly strong rye flavor; it is moist, chewy, and rather fine-grained.

Dissolve yeast in ½ cup of the warm water. Add remaining 4 cups water, shortening, salt, molasses, rye meal, and 2 cups all-purpose flour. Stir to blend. Let rise 1 hour until foamy.

Add remaining 6 cups all-purpose flour and knead until smooth, working in additional flour if needed. Divide dough in half, place in 2 greased 8½-inch loaf pans, and let rise until doubled. Bake in preheated 350°F oven for 50 to 60 minutes, or until tests done.

Yield: Two 8½-inch loaves.

*Sarah Elmendorf
Peru, New York*

CARAWAY-RYE BREAD

ဆ

3 tablespoons granulated sugar
2 tablespoons brown sugar
1 tablespoon salt
2½ cups lukewarm water
2 tablespoons molasses
2 cakes yeast or 2 packages
    (2 tablespoons) dry yeast
2 tablespoons shortening
1 cup rye flour
2 tablespoons caraway seeds
6 to 6¼ cups unbleached
    all-purpose flour

Of all the breads I serve to our bed-and-breakfast guests, this continues to be one of the favorites. It is especially good toasted and spread with homemade raspberry jam, or used for a ham sandwich.

Mix sugars and salt together. Add water, molasses, and yeast, and stir until dissolved. Mix in shortening, rye flour, and caraway seeds, blending well. Add enough all-purpose flour to make dough easy to handle.

Turn out onto floured board and knead, adding more flour as needed, until smooth and elastic. Place in greased bowl, turning to grease top. Cover and let rise in warm place until doubled in bulk.

Punch down dough and let rise again. Punch down and

divide dough in half. Place in 2 greased 9-inch loaf pans and let rise once more. Bake in preheated 375°F oven for 30 to 40 minutes, depending on how brown you like your bread.

Yield: Two 9-inch loaves.

Donna Hodge
Frankenmuth, Michigan

CLARA LYDELL'S RYE BREAD

1 package (1 tablespoon)
  dry yeast
¼ teaspoon granulated sugar
½ cup lukewarm water
½ cup molasses
⅓ cup margarine
¼ cup brown sugar
¼ cup granulated sugar
1 teaspoon salt
3 teaspoons fennel seeds or
  caraway seeds, crushed, or
  1½ teaspoons each (optional)
1 cup boiling water
1 cup lukewarm water
2½ cups rye flour
4 to 5 cups unbleached
  all-purpose flour

This is the only yeast bread I remember my grandmother making. One year while I was in college, I decided it was time for this family favorite to be written down, so I watched her, translating her broken-handled coffee-cup measurements into standard measures and noting her comments: if you have dark molasses, use less; if you want a sweet bread, use more white sugar; if you want a softer bread, use a little more lard or oleo; you'll need about twice as much white flour as rye flour. Now I make it for my daughter—it's her favorite.

Dissolve yeast and ¼ teaspoon granulated sugar in ½ cup lukewarm water; stir and set aside. In large bowl, combine molasses, margarine, brown sugar, ¼ cup granulated sugar, salt, and seeds (if using). Add boiling water and stir to melt margarine and dissolve sugars. Add 1 cup lukewarm water, yeast mixture, and rye flour, beating until well mixed. Stir in all-purpose flour, turn out dough onto floured surface, and knead; dough will be sticky. Cover and let rise in warm place until doubled. Punch down, place in 2 greased 9-inch loaf pans, and let rise again. Bake in preheated 350°F oven for about 45 minutes.

Yield: Two 9-inch loaves.

Diane Nelson
Ames, Iowa

NORWEGIAN SWEET BREAD

2 packages (2 tablespoons)
   dry yeast
1¼ cups warm milk
6 cups unbleached
   all-purpose flour
½ cup honey
1 tablespoon salt
½ teaspoon cloves
½ teaspoon black pepper
1 bottle (12 ounces) beer
½ cup light corn syrup
1 egg
2 cups rye flour
1 cup raisins

A unique sweet-and-spicy bread with a soft, chewy texture. Good with meals or as a snack.

In large bowl, stir yeast into milk. Add all-purpose flour, honey, salt, cloves, pepper, beer, corn syrup, and egg, and beat until well blended. Cover and set aside for 40 minutes.

Stir in rye flour and raisins, turn out onto floured surface, and knead dough until smooth. Let rise until doubled, punch down, and let rest 10 minutes. Divide into 3 loaves and place in greased 9-inch loaf pans. Let rise until doubled.

Bake in preheated 375°F oven for about 40 minutes. (Cover tops with foil for last 20 minutes if they begin to brown too much.)

Yield: Three 9-inch loaves.

Susan Holec
Evansville, Wisconsin

BEER BREAD

1 cup whole-wheat flour
2 packages (2 tablespoons)
   dry yeast
1 bottle (12 ounces) dark beer
½ cup water
2 tablespoons honey
¼ cup sorghum or molasses
3 tablespoons oil
4 to 4½ cups unbleached
   all-purpose flour
Melted margarine (optional)

This sweet, flavorful bread needs no salt or eggs, which makes it good for those on low-salt and low-cholesterol diets. I started baking this bread after my husband's heart attack and found it was tasty enough for the whole family to enjoy.

Combine whole-wheat flour and yeast in small bowl. Heat beer, water, honey, sorghum, and oil in saucepan to 120°F. Add flour-and-yeast mixture and beat well with wire whisk. Add all-purpose flour, 1 cup at a time, until dough can be handled. Turn out onto floured surface and knead well. Place dough in greased bowl, cover, and let rise until doubled in bulk. Punch down and let rise again.

Divide dough into 2 pieces, shape each into round loaf,

and place on greased baking sheet. With sharp knife, make a shallow slash across each loaf. Let rise until doubled. Bake in preheated 350°F oven about 40 minutes, or until loaves sound hollow when tapped. Brush with melted margarine if a soft crust is desired.

Yield: Two 8-inch round loaves.

Gloria Wiech
Frontenac, Minnesota

CJ's E-Z HERB BREAD

ɞ

¾ cup boiling water
¾ cup evaporated milk
1 teaspoon poppy seeds
1 teaspoon caraway seeds
1 teaspoon instant minced onion
1 teaspoon dried chervil or parsley
½ teaspoon dried marjoram or
  oregano
2 tablespoons sugar
2 teaspoons salt
  (or less to taste)
4 tablespoons margarine
2 packages (2 tablespoons)
  dry yeast
½ cup warm water
2 eggs, well beaten
4 to 4½ cups sifted
  whole-wheat flour
Melted butter
Salt (optional)

Our family has always had a love affair with the "staff of life" in all its many variations. We have enjoyed trying new and unusual recipes, but we still return to this lovely herb bread for all occasions.

Combine boiling water and evaporated milk. (Note that 1½ cups warm water may be substituted for the evaporated milk and boiling water.) Add seeds, onion, herbs, sugar, and 2 teaspoons salt. Stir in margarine and cool to lukewarm.

Dissolve yeast in warm water and stir into milk mixture. Add eggs and flour, and beat vigorously for 2 minutes. Cover and let rise in warm place until more than doubled in bulk.

Stir down with spoon, beating hard again for 2 minutes. Turn into round, liberally greased 2-quart baking dish or casserole dish. Let rise for 5 to 10 minutes. Bake in preheated 350 to 375°F oven for 40 to 45 minutes. Brush with butter and sprinkle sparingly with salt of any grade, if desired.

Yield: One 8-inch round loaf.

Cora L. T. Johnson
Smithfield, Utah

WHOLE-WHEAT HERB BRAID

&

1½ cups lukewarm water
2 packages (2 tablespoons)
   dry yeast
1 tablespoon salt
1 tablespoon rosemary
½ tablespoon thyme
7 cups stone-ground
   whole-wheat flour
1 cup milk
1 tablespoon butter or
   margarine
½ cup unbleached all-purpose
   flour for kneading
   (approximately)
1 egg, beaten
Sesame seeds

This is a bread I created to complement Thanksgiving dinner. I also make it for our volunteer potluck dinner at our local folk music coffeehouse—the Godfrey Daniels. It is eye-catching and always disappears quickly.

Pour water in large warmed bowl. Sprinkle yeast over water and stir until dissolved. Cover and let stand 15 minutes.

Combine salt, rosemary, thyme, and 2½ cups of the whole-wheat flour. Beat into yeast mixture for 2 minutes. Heat milk and butter until very warm but not hot. Add to yeast mixture and beat 2 minutes. Add 1 cup whole-wheat flour to make a thick batter and beat 2 minutes. Stir in remaining whole-wheat flour to form a soft, sticky dough. Turn into greased bowl, cover, and let rise in warm place until doubled (about 1½ hours).

Punch down dough, turn out onto floured surface, and knead until smooth and elastic, about 10 minutes, adding all-purpose flour as needed. Divide dough into 3 equal pieces, roll into ropes, and braid. (Dough may be divided into 6 equal pieces for two smaller loaves.) Place on baking sheet, cover, and let rise in warm place until doubled (about 30 minutes).

Brush top of loaf or loaves with beaten egg and sprinkle generously with sesame seeds. Bake in preheated 450°F oven for 30 to 35 minutes, or until it sounds hollow when tapped. Cool on rack.

Yield: 1 large loaf or 2 small loaves.

Donna Mutchler
Bethlehem, Pennsylvania

SANDWICH BREAD

2

1 package (1 tablespoon)
 dry yeast
¼ cup warm water
2 tablespoons sugar
1½ teaspoons salt
¾ cup hot water
1½ tablespoons finely chopped
 onion
2½ tablespoons finely chopped
 green pepper
2½ tablespoons finely chopped,
 drained pimiento
3 to 3½ cups unbleached
 all-purpose flour

This is a colorful and tasty bread that goes well with homemade soup or chili and makes excellent sandwiches.

Dissolve yeast in ¼ cup warm water and set aside.

In large bowl, combine sugar, salt, ¾ cup hot water, onion, green pepper, and pimiento. Cool mixture to lukewarm and mix in 1 cup flour. Stir in softened yeast, add remaining flour, and knead lightly. Let rest 10 minutes.

Turn out onto floured surface and knead 5 to 8 minutes. Place in greased bowl, rotate dough so top is greased, cover, and let rest 10 minutes.

Turn out again and knead until smooth and elastic. Form into loaf and place in 7-inch loaf pan. Let rise until doubled. Bake in preheated 375°F oven for 40 to 45 minutes.

Yield: One 7-inch loaf.

Betty Clifton
Three Rivers, Michigan

HEARTY FOCACCIA

ॐ

1 package (1 tablespoon)
  dry yeast
Pinch of turbinado, maple, or
  granulated sugar
1¾ cups warm water
¼ teaspoon coarse salt (optional)
½ teaspoon freshly ground
  black pepper
5 tablespoons olive oil
3½ to 4½ cups multigrain flour
  (or mixture of whole-wheat
  and all-purpose)
Chopped fresh rosemary (to taste)

A delicious alternative to traditional yeast breads, this performs well as an appetizer, as an accompaniment to Italian dishes, or as a sandwich bread stuffed with caponata, salami, cappicola, mozzarella, roasted peppers, or tomatoes and fresh basil. The delightful hint of rosemary makes it an ideal bread to eat plain, served with just a glass of red wine and fresh mozzarella.

Combine yeast and sugar in large mixing bowl. Stir in ⅓ cup of the warm water, cover with damp cloth, and set aside in warm place for roughly 5 minutes, or until it starts to froth. Add remaining water, salt (if using), pepper, and 3 tablespoons of the oil. Stir in 2 cups of the flour and the fresh rosemary to taste. Add another ½ cup of the flour, or as much as is needed to form a soft dough that can be gathered together.

Turn out dough onto well-floured surface and knead for 8 to 9 minutes, adding flour as needed to keep dough from sticking. Oil large mixing bowl with ½ teaspoon of remaining oil. Roll dough around bowl to lightly coat it with oil. Cover with damp cloth and set aside to rise for 1 hour, or until doubled in bulk.

Oil 1 or 2 baking sheets with some of remaining oil. Cut dough in half, form into 2 small, round loaves, and place on baking sheets. Prick tops in several places with fork, then brush with remaining oil and sprinkle with additional rosemary. Bake in preheated 500°F oven for 20 to 25 minutes, or until focaccia is browned on bottom and lightly browned on top. Cut into quarters and serve warm or cooled to room temperature.

Yield: Two round loaves.

Scott Edward Anderson
Garrison, New York

Parmesan Herb Bread

❧

1 package (1 tablespoon)
  dry yeast
1 teaspoon sugar
1 cup plus 2 tablespoons
  warm water (105 to 115°F)
1 cup mixed fresh herbs (basil,
  oregano, parsley, cilantro, etc.)
3 tablespoons grated
  Parmesan cheese
2 cups unbleached
  all-purpose flour
1 cup bread flour
2 tablespoons olive oil
1 teaspoon salt
1 teaspoon cracked pepper
Cornmeal
1 teaspoon flour
  (for top of loaves)

Fresh herbs are a must in this enticing, distinctively flavored bread. Serve hot with pasta or as a snack, slathered with butter.

Stir yeast and sugar into warm water and set aside until foamy, about 5 minutes.

Mince herbs and combine in large bowl with Parmesan cheese, flours, oil, salt, and pepper. Make a well in center and pour in yeast mixture, working it into other ingredients.

Turn out onto floured surface and knead until elastic and smooth (about 10 minutes). Place dough in large plastic bag and seal top (squeezing out all the air first). Place in bowl and let rise in warm spot for 1 hour and 15 minutes.

Punch dough down, cut in half, and form into 2 baguettes. Place on oiled baking sheet sprinkled with cornmeal, cover with piece of oiled plastic wrap, oiled side down, and let rise 1 more hour.

Sift 1 teaspoon flour over top of loaves, then bake in preheated 375°F oven until golden brown, about 30 minutes. (Loaves should sound hollow when tapped on bottom.) Cool on wire rack.

Yield: 2 baguettes.

Debbie Fifles
Evanston, Illinois

FRENCH BREAD STROMBOLLI XPRESS

੨◑

4½ to 5 cups bread flour
1 tablespoon sugar
1 tablespoon salt
2 packages (2 tablespoons)
   dry yeast
1 tablespoon margarine
1¾ cups warm water (125°F)
Filling of choice
Softened margarine
Grated or sliced cheese

My family loves this meal-within-a-bread and requests it often. The variations of fillings are endless—leftovers, chicken, beans, etc. Great for picnics, lunches, and get-togethers with friends.

In large bowl, combine 1½ cups of the flour, sugar, salt, yeast, and margarine. Gradually add warm water, beating 2 minutes at medium speed. Add ¾ cup flour and beat on high an additional 2 minutes. Stir in about 2 cups flour, then turn out onto floured surface and knead 7 to 10 minutes.

Shape into ball, cover with plastic wrap, then towel, and let rest for 20 minutes.

Divide dough into 2 pieces and roll out on floured surface into rectangular shape. Fill with one of the following or try a different filling for each:

Filling # 1: Spread with mustard, leaving 1 inch around all sides. Add ham and cheese slices, chopped garlic, onions, green peppers, and tomatoes. Sprinkle with salt, pepper, and parsley flakes.

Filling # 2: Sprinkle with cooked and crumbled Italian sausage. Add mozzarella cheese, chopped garlic, onions, and green peppers. Sprinkle with oregano and spread with spaghetti sauce.

Filling # 3: Add chopped broccoli and tomatoes, cooked egg slices, and Muenster and Swiss cheese slices.

After filling bread, roll it up, starting on longer side, to make a loaf. Place on greased baking sheet. Rub softened margarine on top of loaves, wrap loosely with plastic wrap, and refrigerate for 2 to 24 hours.

When ready to bake, remove from refrigerator, discard plastic wrap, and let dough rest for 10 minutes.

Bake in preheated 375°F oven for 20 to 25 minutes, or until

golden brown. Remove from baking sheets, place on serving platter, and sprinkle with grated cheese or top with sliced cheese. Let rest for 10 minutes.

Yield: 2 loaves.

Michele Bryant
Orlando, Florida

FRENCH BREAD

ﾠ

6 to 7 cups unbleached
   all-purpose flour
2 packages (2 tablespoons)
   dry yeast
2½ cups water
2 tablespoons sugar
1 tablespoon salt
1 tablespoon shortening
Cornmeal
1 egg white, beaten
1 tablespoon water
Sesame seeds (optional)

This crunchy, smooth-textured bread is delightful anytime—for meals, snacks, and gifts to family and friends.

In large bowl, mix 3 cups of the flour and the yeast. Heat water, sugar, salt, and shortening until warm, stirring constantly until shortening melts. Cool (to 115 to 120°F) and add to flour mixture, beating for about 3 minutes. Stir in 2½ cups flour. Turn out onto floured surface and knead for about 8 to 10 minutes, until dough is shiny, working in about 1 cup more of remaining flour. Place in lightly greased bowl, cover, and let rise until doubled.

Punch down and divide into 2 equal pieces. Form each into 12x15-inch rectangle and roll up from long edge, tucking under ends. Place on baking sheet sprinkled with cornmeal and brush with egg white combined with 1 tablespoon water. Allow to rise until doubled (about 1 hour).

Slash diagonal lines on top for ease in pulling baked bread apart. Brush again with egg-white mixture and sprinkle sesame seeds on top, if desired. Bake in preheated 375°F oven for 20 minutes, brush again with egg-white mixture, and bake 20 minutes longer. Cool.

Yield: 2 loaves.

Joyce M. Alvernaz
Paso Robles, California

DILLY CASSEROLE BREAD

ès

1 package (1 tablespoon)
  dry yeast
¼ cup warm water (110 to 115°F)
1 cup cottage cheese
  at room temperature
2 tablespoons sugar
1 tablespoon minced onion
1 tablespoon butter or
  margarine, melted (or oil)
2 tablespoons dill seed
1 teaspoon salt
¼ teaspoon baking soda
1 egg
2¼ to 2½ cups unbleached
  all-purpose flour (or substitute
  ⅓ with whole-wheat flour)
Butter

This savory bread is almost a meal in itself. Serve with homemade soup or stew.

Mix yeast in water and set aside. In mixing bowl, combine cottage cheese, sugar, onion, 1 tablespoon melted butter, dill seed, salt, soda, and egg, beating until blended. Stir in softened yeast. Gradually add flour to form stiff dough. Cover and let rise in warm place for about 1 hour.

Stir down dough and turn into well-greased 8-inch round casserole dish (about 1½- to 2-quart size). Let rise 30 to 40 minutes. Bake in preheated 350°F oven for 35 to 45 minutes. Brush with butter and cut in wedges to serve.

Yield: 10 servings.

Doris Byers
Bargersville, Indiana

BRAIDED DILL BREAD

ès

1 package (1 tablespoon)
  dry yeast
¼ cup warm water
1 cup sour cream
1 egg
1 tablespoon dried onion
2 tablespoons sugar
1 tablespoon butter, melted
(continued)

A beautiful golden-brown braided bread with a light texture, firm crust, and burst of flavor from the dill seed. Economical in time and money.

In large bowl, dissolve yeast in warm water. Mix sour cream, egg, onion, sugar, butter, salt, and dill seed in small bowl. Microwave until lukewarm. Add to yeast mixture, stir in 1 cup flour, and beat. Add enough flour to make soft dough and knead until smooth and elastic, about 6 to 8 minutes.

Place in greased bowl and cover with plastic wrap. Let rise in warm place until doubled. Punch down and divide into 3 equal balls. Roll each ball into rope about 18 inches long.
(continued)

1 teaspoon salt
1 tablespoon dill seed
3 to 3½ cups unbleached
  all-purpose flour

Braid the 3 ropes together, place on greased baking sheet, and cover with plastic wrap. Let rise until doubled.

Bake in preheated 350°F oven for 35 to 40 minutes. Cover lightly with foil after 10 to 15 minutes to prevent overbrowning.

Yield: 1 loaf.

Darlene Wright
Peru, Nebraska

SAVORY DILL BREAD

❧

2 cups small-curd
  cottage cheese
2 tablespoons butter
¼ cup sugar
2 teaspoons salt
¼ cup minced onion
½ cup dill weed
½ teaspoon baking soda
2 eggs
2 packages (2 tablespoons)
  dry yeast
½ cup warm water
  (100 to 110°F)
½ teaspoon sugar
5 cups unbleached
  all-purpose flour
Butter

Easy to prepare, this flavorful bread is especially good for sandwiches.

Heat cottage cheese with 2 tablespoons butter until barely lukewarm. Combine with ¼ cup sugar, salt, onion, dill, soda, and eggs in large bowl. Dissolve yeast in warm water with ½ teaspoon sugar, and as soon as mixture turns bubbly, stir into cottage-cheese mixture. Add flour all at once and blend thoroughly. Let rise until doubled.

Punch down dough and turn into 2 well-greased 9-inch loaf pans. Let rise until barely doubled and bake in preheated 350°F oven for 50 minutes. Butter tops while warm.

Yield: Two 9-inch loaves.

Dave Sonderschafer
Skandia, Michigan

SOURDOUGH BREAD I

&

SOURDOUGH STARTER
1 cup water reserved from
  boiling potatoes (no salt)
1½ to 2½ cups whole-wheat flour
  (or more, as needed)

BREAD
2 cups Sourdough Starter
3½ cups warm water
4 to 6 cups unbleached
  all-purpose flour
¼ cup warm water
2 packages (2 tablespoons)
  dry yeast
2 tablespoons salt
4 to 6 cups unbleached
  all-purpose flour
Cornmeal

You need to plan ahead when making this if you don't have the starter on hand, which requires about 10 days before it's ready for use. Once you have some experience with sourdough bread, start experimenting with different flours and grains, as they create a distinctive texture. This bread is very moist and chewy. Enjoy!

To make the starter, mix potato water with 1½ cups whole-wheat flour in ceramic, glass, or plastic bowl (metal container should not be used) and let stand uncovered for a few days. If top gets dry, stir mixture, adding another cup or so of flour to make soft dough. Cover and let stand an additional 5 to 7 days (total time is about 10 days).

The night before making bread, mix sourdough starter with 3½ cups warm water, then add flour, 1 cup at a time. Mix well and incorporate lots of air. The end result should be a thick batter-like dough. Let stand for at least 12 hours in warm place, covered.

The next morning, remove about 2 cups of this mixture to use as your new sourdough starter. Store in cool place, covered, until ready for your next bread-baking session.

To the remaining mix, add ¼ cup warm water, the yeast, salt, and flour, 1 cup at a time, mixing well after each addition. When dough becomes too heavy to work with a spoon, turn out onto floured surface and knead for about 10 minutes, until smooth and elastic, not sticky. Place dough in oiled bowl and rotate so entire surface is oiled. Let stand, covered, in warm place until doubled in bulk (about 2 hours).

Punch dough down, shape into 2 free-form loaves, and put on baking sheet covered with cornmeal (or place in 2 nonstick 9-inch loaf pans). Sprinkle with warm water, slash tops of loaves, and let sit until doubled (about 30 minutes).

(continued)

Preheat oven to 425°F and place an empty pan on bottom shelf. (Oven must be hot when you start baking bread.) Put bread in oven and pour a cup of water into hot, empty pan on bottom shelf (be very careful of the steam generated and close the oven quickly to keep the steam in). Bake about 30 to 40 minutes (the water will have evaporated after about 30 minutes; if not, remove the pan from oven).

Yield: 2 loaves.

Andrea Beer
Anoka, Minnesota

SOURDOUGH STARTER

ðŸ‚Ž

1 package (1 tablespoon)
  dry yeast
½ cup warm water
1½ cups warm water
2 cups unbleached
  all-purpose flour

When a sourdough starter is "resting," cover the top with a dish towel, cheesecloth, or wax paper, for it needs to be able to "breathe." The batch you save for future use or share with another person should be at least 1½ cups.

Two to 4 days ahead, dissolve yeast in ½ cup warm water. Stir and let sit 5 minutes. In nonmetal bowl (1½- to 2-quart size) combine 1½ cups warm water, flour, and yeast mixture. Stir or whisk until smooth. Let sit in warm spot (65 to 75°F) lightly covered for at least 2 days. Mixture will bubble a lot, develop a pleasant, sour, yeasty aroma, and may eventually separate with a clear liquid on top. The starter is now ready to use or store for later use.

Diane Koss
Burlington, Vermont

SOURDOUGH BREAD II

2½ cups flour
2 cups milk or water
2 cups lukewarm water
1 package (1 tablespoon)
    dry yeast
1 cup sourdough starter
    (your own favorite)
⅓ cup sugar
1 teaspoon salt
7 to 8 cups unbleached
    all-purpose flour
1 egg yolk, beaten
1 tablespoon water

In 1980, I received a "gift" from my future mother-in-law: a sourdough starter. I had no idea what to do with it, but I began to research the subject, for if she wanted me to bake bread for her son, I'd at least have to give it a try! My sourdough starter dates back to my husband's grandmother, Maxine Lawrence Presley, who passed it on to her daughter-in-law, Carolyn Helman. All the books and articles I've read hold differing opinions about sourdough. I figured that Maxine, who was an Oregon pioneer, would know more than the books, so I keep my starter according to the information I learned from her. Some sources say you are supposed to "feed" your sourdough water and flour; Maxine used milk. Milk, I have found, adds to the sour taste, and I have yet to "kill" my starter (which is impossible, anyway)! You can keep your own starter any way you like. This bread recipe is an adaptation of a sourdough roll recipe of Carolyn's.

The night before, add 2½ cups flour and 2 cups milk to your sourdough starter and let sit out overnight. This feeds the starter. The next day, mix together lukewarm water and yeast in large bowl and let sit 5 minutes. Add sourdough starter, sugar, and salt to yeast mixture, and stir well. Stir in 5 cups of the flour, creating a sticky dough. Cover with warm, damp cloth and set in warm place to rise, about 60 minutes.

Punch down dough and add enough remaining flour to make dough workable. Knead until pliable, divide, and knead again. Shape into 2 large round or oval loaves and place each on greased baking sheet. Let rise until doubled in bulk. Slash tops with sharp knife or razor blade and baste with egg yolk combined with 1 tablespoon water. Bake in preheated 350°F oven for 30 to 35 minutes.

Yield: 2 loaves.

Jaci Presley
Beavercreek, Oregon

HOLIDAY STOLLEN

ॐ

¾ cup mixed candied fruit
½ cup raisins
2 tablespoons rum
5½ to 6½ cups unbleached
   all-purpose flour
½ cup sugar
1¼ teaspoons salt
2 packages (2 tablespoons)
   dry yeast
1¼ cups milk
½ cup (1 stick) butter or
   margarine
3 eggs at room temperature
¾ cup chopped almonds
1 cup confectioners' sugar
1 tablespoon water
Sliced almonds
Candied cherries

Great for Christmas, this lovely bread has a fine-grained texture complemented by the crunch of almonds and chewiness of candied fruit. If covered with plastic wrap, it needs only a bow to be an attractive—as well as a delicious—gift.

Combine candied fruit, raisins, and rum, and set aside. In large bowl of mixer, stir together 2 cups of the flour, sugar, salt, and yeast until well mixed. Heat milk and butter until very warm (120 to 130°F); butter does not need to melt completely. Gradually add to flour mixture and beat 2 minutes, scraping bowl occasionally. Add eggs and ½ cup flour, or enough to make a thick batter. Beat at high speed for 2 minutes, scraping bowl occasionally. Stir in enough remaining flour to make a soft dough.

Turn out onto generously floured surface and knead 8 to 10 minutes, or until smooth and elastic. Place in greased bowl and turn to grease top. Cover and let rise in warm, draft-free place until doubled, about 1½ hours.

Punch down dough, turn out onto floured surface, and knead in fruit mixture and chopped almonds. Divide into 3 equal pieces and roll each to about a 7x12-inch oval. Fold each in half lengthwise and place on greased baking sheets. Cover and let rise in warm, draft-free place until doubled.

Bake in preheated 350°F oven for 20 to 25 minutes, or until bread tests done. Cool slightly on racks.

To make frosting, beat together confectioners' sugar and water until smooth. Spread on tops of stolen and decorate with sliced almonds and cherries. Remove from racks and cool completely. Wrap and store in cool place. Will keep 3 days.

Yield: 3 loaves.

Emily McHugh
Chestertown, New York

INDEX

— ❧ —

A
❧

Alice's Brown Bread, 167
Almonds
  Almond & Poppy-Seed
    Muffins, 99
  Almond Butter Cookies, 75
  Almond Chocolate Torte, 47
  Holiday Stollen, 215
Angel Flake Biscuits, 118
Anne's Oatmeal
  Cookies, 71, *134*
Apples
  Apple-Raisin Bread Braid,
    184
  Apple Surprise Muffins, 100
  Applesauce Cake with
    Caramel Icing, 58
  Company Pie, 16, *53*

English Apple Pudding
  Cake, 59
Golden Delicious Apple
  Cake, 57
Granny Smith Coffee
  Cake, 62
Hearty Apple Cake, 60
Honey Apple Pie, 11
Joan Pearson's Apple
  Muffins, 99
Morning-Glory Bread, 157
Oats & Applesauce Muffins,
  100
Prize-Winning Applesauce
  Cake, 57
Seasonal Fruitcake, 65
Special Muffins, 101
Stained-Glass Pie, 15
Sugarless Apple Pie, 11, *56*

Apricots
  Apricot Bars, 93
  Apricot Bread, 152
  Apricot Pastry Hearts, *49*, 83
  Apricot-Pecan Bread, 185
  Apricot-Raisin-Bran Bread,
    152
  Stained-Glass Pie, 15

B
❧

Babka, 64
Baking Powder Biscuits, 118
Bananas
  Banana & Sour-Cream
    Bread, 153
  Banana Muffins, 103

Fresh Ginger Banana Bread, 154
Raspberry Honey Banana Muffins, 103, *135*
Unconventional Fruitcake, 39
Basil Pound Cake, 41
Bean & Butter Bread, 178
Beer Bread, 202
Best-Ever Brownies, 96
Biscuits, Buns & Rolls
Angel Flake Biscuits, 118
Baking Powder Biscuits, 118
Butterhorns, 127, *129*
Buttermilk Rolls, 138
Caramel Rolls, 142
Cheese Crescents, 137
Cinnamon Buns, 125
Creamed-Corn Biscuits, 121
Easy Buttermilk Biscuits, 119
Easy Sesame Breadsticks or Buns, *54*, 124
Fabulous Crescent Rolls, 128
Favorite Buttermilk Rolls, 138
Featherbed Rolls, 139
Glazed Orange Rolls, 144
Golden Onion Rolls, 149
Grandma's Fluffy Buns, 122
Jiffy Hamburger Buns, 123
Mashed-Potato Refrigerator Rolls, 147
Master Mix for Southern Biscuits, 119
Mom's Easy Cinnamon Rolls, 141
Mrs. L's Buttermilk Biscuits, *52*, 120
My Favorite Biscuits, 117
Oat-Bran Rolls, *129*, 148
Old-Fashioned Hot Cross Buns, 126
Orange Swirl Rolls, 143
Pecan Sticky Buns, 125
Rich Shortcake Biscuits, 120
Rich Yeast Rolls, 146

Sour Cream Twists, 145
Swedish Rolls, 140
Whole-Wheat Rolls, 146
Black Forest Cheesecake, 29, *132*
Black Raspberry Muffins, 108
Black-Bottom Cups, 110
Blackberry Jam Cake, 32
Blonde Brownies, 96
Blueberries
Blueberry Buttermilk Muffins, 105
Blueberry Coffee Cake, *50*, 63
Blueberry Pie, 12
Cherry-Berry Pie, 21
Never-Fail Blueberry Muffins, 104
North Woods Muffins, 101
The Very, Very Best Blueberry Muffins, 104
Boston Brown-Bread Muffins, 112
Braided Dill Bread, 210
Breads, *see Quick Breads, Yeast Breads*
Brenda's Bran Muffins, 113
Brown-Sugar Oatmeal Muffins, 102
Brownies
Best-Ever Brownies, 96
Blonde Brownies, 96
Buckwheat Bread, 182
Buns, *see Biscuits, Buns & Rolls*
Butterhorns, 127, *129*
Buttermilk
Angel Flake Biscuits, 118
Blueberry Buttermilk Muffins, 105
Boston Brown-Bread Muffins, 112
Buttermilk Rolls, 138
Buttermilk-Herb-Tomato Bread, 168
Carrot Corn Bread, 169
Eagles Bread, 187

Easy Buttermilk Biscuits, 119
Favorite Buttermilk Rolls, 138
Graham-Flour Bread, 190
Irish Freckle Bread, 166
Lillie's Gingerbread Muffins, 111
Mrs. L's Buttermilk Biscuits, *52*, 120
North Woods Muffins, 101
Orange-Chocolate Muffins, 110, *135*
Quick Cinnamon Bread, 151
Rhubarb Bread, 162
Rhubarb Muffins, 109
Winter-Squash Muffins, 113

C

Cakes
Almond Chocolate Torte, 47
Applesauce Cake with Caramel Icing, 58
Babka, 64
Basil Pound Cake, 41
Black Forest Cheesecake, 29, *132*
Blackberry Jam Cake, 32
Blueberry Coffee Cake, *50*, 63
Chiffon Cake, 32, *51*
Choco-Dot Pumpkin Cake, 60
Chocolate Cake with Fluffy Coconut Frosting, 46, *131*
Company Cheesecake, 31
Crustless Chocolate Cheesecake, 30

Date Cake with Choco-
  Nut Topping, 43
English Apple Pudding
  Cake, 59
Fruit Coffee Cake, 66
Golden Delicious Apple
  Cake, 57
Gramma Freda's Oatmeal
  Cake, 40
Grandma Nelson's Cake, 48
Grandmama Strouse's
  Coconut Cream Cake, 42
Granny Smith Coffee
  Cake, 62
Greek Walnut Cakes, 36
Hearty Apple Cake, 60
Hungarian Coffee Cake, 68
Kiss-Me Cake, 38
Oatmeal Chocolate Cake, 45
Orange Cake, 33
Orange Carrot Cake, 37
Peaches & Cheese Cake, 34
Pound Cake, 40
Prize-Winning Applesauce
  Cake, 57
Prune Cake, 39
Pumpkin Cake Roll, 61
Raspberry Cream-Cheese
  Coffee Cake, 67
Refrigerator Coffee Cake, 69
Rhubarb Coffee Cake, 62
Seasonal Fruitcake, 65
Special-Treat Cheesecake, 35
Twenty-Minute Fudge
  Cake, 44
Unconventional Fruitcake, 39
California Squaw Bread, 173
Caramel Rolls, 142
Caramel-Topped Squash Pie, 19
Caraway-Rye Bread, 200
Carrots
  Carrot Corn Bread, 169
  Carrot-Nut Bread, 160
  Morning-Glory Bread, 157
  Orange Carrot Cake, 37

Special Muffins, 101
Cattern Cakes, 79
Cheesecake, see *Cakes*
Cherries
  Black Forest Cheesecake,
    29, *132*
  Cherry Bread, 156
  Cherry-Berry Pie, 21
Chewy Granola Bars, 95
Chiffon Cake, 32, *51*
Choco-Dot Pumpkin Cake, 60
Chocolate
  Almond Chocolate Torte, 47
  Best-Ever Brownies, 96
  Black Forest Cheesecake,
    29, *132*
  Black-Bottom Cups, 110
  Blonde Brownies, 96
  Choco-Dot Pumpkin Cake,
    60
  Chocolate Cake with Fluffy
    Coconut Frosting, 46, *131*
  Chocolate Pie, 23
  Chocolate Zucchini Bread,
    164
  Crustless Chocolate
    Cheesecake, 30
  Date Cake with Choco-
    Nut Topping, 43
  Grandma's Cookies, 72
  Magic Peanut Butter
    Middles, 73
  Oatmeal Chocolate Cake, 45
  Oatmeal-Raisin Chocolate-
    Chip Cookies, 76
  Oh Henry Bars, 94
  Orange-Chocolate Muffins,
    110, *135*
  Pecan Fudge Pie, 24
  Prize-Winning Applesauce
    Cake, 57
  Sinbad Bars, 94, *133*
  Spicy Oatmeal & Choco-
    late-Chip Cookies, 77
  Texas Buffalo Chips, 72

Tweed Squares, 97
Twenty-Minute Fudge
  Cake, 44
Christmas Casserole Cookies, 88
Christmas Thimble Cookies, 82
Cindy's Wheatberry Bread, 192
Cinnamon Buns, 125
CJ's E-Z Herb Bread, 203
Clara Lydell's Rye Bread, 201
Coconut
  Chocolate Cake with Fluffy
    Coconut Frosting, 46, *131*
  Christmas Casserole
    Cookies, 88
  Fresh Coconut Pie, 20
  Gramma Freda's Oatmeal
    Cake, 40
  Grandmama Strouse's
    Coconut Cream Cake, 42
  Morning-Glory Bread, 157
  Oatmeal Pie, 17
  Orange Carrot Cake, 37
  Raspberry Bars, 91, *133*
Company Cheesecake, 31
Company Pie, 16, *53*
Cookies & Bars
  Almond Butter Cookies, 75
  Anne's Oatmeal Cookies,
    71, *134*
  Apricot Bars, 93
  Apricot Pastry Hearts, *49*, 83
  Best-Ever Brownies, 96
  Blonde Brownies, 96
  Cattern Cakes, 79
  Chewy Granola Bars, 95
  Christmas Casserole
    Cookies, 88
  Christmas Thimble
    Cookies, 82
  Crybaby Cookies, 80
  Date-Filled Cookies, 86, *130*
  Easy Peanut Butter
    Cookies, 74
  Family Treasure
    Butterhorns, 84

Famous Peanut Butter
    Cookies, 74
Gingersnaps, 81
Grandma's Cookies, 72
Hazelnut Meringues, 87
Hermits, 90
Jam Bars, 90
Janhagel Cookies, 87
Kifle Cookies, 84, *134*
Lemon Bars, 89
Lemon Oatmeal Cookies, 71
Magic Peanut Butter
    Middles, 73
Oatmeal-Raisin Chocolate-
    Chip Cookies, 76
Oh Henry Bars, 94
Pecan Praline Cookies, 78
Persimmon Cookies, 82
Pistachio Icebox Cookies, 78
Raspberry Bars, 91, *133*
Shortbread, 88
Sinbad Bars, 94, *133*
Spicy Oatmeal & Choco-
    late-Chip Cookies, 77
Surprise Cookies, 80
Texas Buffalo Chips, 72
Tweed Squares, 97
Yummy Rhubarb Squares, 92
Cornmeal
    Boston Brown-Bread
        Muffins, 112
    Carrot Corn Bread, 169
    Early Colonial Bread, 196
    Massachusetts Anadama
        Bread, 194
    Mexican Corn Bread, *55*, 169
    Squash Spoon Bread, 168
    Sundial Farm Anadama
        Bread, 195
Cranberries
    Company Pie, 16, *53*
    Cranberry Bread with
        Cream Cheese, 159
    Cranberry Date-Nut Bread,
        158

Cranberry, Walnut &
    Orange Muffins, 106
    Cranberry-Orange Bread, 159
    North Woods Muffins, 101
    Stained-Glass Pie, 15
Creamed-Corn Biscuits, 121
Crunchy-Top Peach Pie, 13
Crustless Chocolate
    Cheesecake, 30
Crybaby Cookies, 80

D

Dates
    Christmas Casserole
        Cookies, 88
    Cranberry Date-Nut Bread,
        158
    Date Cake with Choco-
        Nut Topping, 43
    Date-Filled Cookies, 86, *130*
    Date-Nut Bread, 155
Dill
    Braided Dill Bread, 210
    Dilly Casserole Bread, 210
    Savory Dill Bread, 211

E

Eagles Bread, 187
Early Colonial Bread, 196
Easy Buttermilk Biscuits, 119
Easy Peanut Butter Cookies, 74
Easy Sesame Breadsticks or
    Buns, *54*, 124
English Apple Pudding Cake, 59
Everyone's Favorite Braided
    Bread, 198

F

Fabulous Crescent Rolls, 128
Family Treasure Butterhorns, 84

Famous Peanut Butter
    Cookies, 74
Favorite All-Purpose Bread, 175
Favorite Buttermilk Rolls, 138
Featherbed Rolls, 139
French Bread, 209
French Bread Strombolli
    Xpress, 208
Fresh Coconut Pie, 20
Fresh Ginger Banana Bread, 154
Fruit Coffee Cake, 66

G

Ginger
    Fresh Ginger Banana Bread,
        154
    Gingersnaps, 81
    Lillie's Gingerbread
        Muffins, 111
Glazed Orange Rolls, 144
Golden Delicious Apple Cake, 57
Golden Onion Rolls, 149
Good Muffins, 112
Graham-Flour Bread, 190
Gramma Freda's Oatmeal
    Cake, 40
Grandma Nelson's Cake, 48
Grandma's Cookies, 72
Grandma's Fluffy Buns, 122
Grandma's Oatmeal Bread, 166
Grandmama Strouse's Coconut
    Cream Cake, 42
Granny Smith Coffee Cake, 62
Grape-Nuts Bread, 165
Greek Walnut Cakes, 36
Grossmutter's Rye-Meal
    Bread, 200

H

Hazelnut Meringues, 87
Health Bread, 197
Hearty Apple Cake, 60

Hearty Focaccia, 206
Hermits, 90
High-Protein Honey Wheat
    Bread, 191
Holiday Stollen, 215
Honey
    Crunchy-Top Peach Pie, 13
    Health Bread, 197
    High-Protein Honey Wheat
        Bread, 191
    Honey Apple Pie, 11
    Honey Peach Pie, 14
    Honey Syrup, 36
    Raspberry Honey Banana
        Muffins, 103, *135*
    Walnut Bread with Allspice
        Butter, 176
Hungarian Coffee Cake, 68

I

Irish Freckle Bread, 166
Italian Wheat Bread, 174

J

Jam Bars, 90
Janhagel Cookies, 87
Jiffy Hamburger Buns, 123
Joan Pearson's Apple Muffins, 99

K

Kifle Cookies, 84, *134*
Kiss-Me Cake, 38

L

Lemon
    Lemon Bars, 89
    Lemon Glaze, 32

Lemon Oatmeal Cookies, 71
Lemon Pie, 22
Lemon Tea Bread, 156
Lillie's Gingerbread Muffins, 111

M

Maggie's Raspberry Muffins, 107
Magic Peanut Butter Middles, 73
Mashed-Potato Refrigerator
    Rolls, 147
Massachusetts Anadama
    Bread, 194
Master Mix for Southern
    Biscuits, 119
Mexican Cornbread, 55, 169
Mike's Potato Whole-Wheat
    Bread, 177
Millmoss Pie (Caramel-Topped
    Squash Pie), 19
Mom's Easy Cinnamon
    Rolls, 141
Morning-Glory Bread, 157
Mountaineer Maple Bread, 186
Mrs. L's Buttermilk Biscuits,
    52, 120
Muffins
    Almond & Poppy-Seed
        Muffins, 99
    Apple Surprise Muffins, 100
    Banana Muffins, 103
    Black Raspberry Muffins, 108
    Black-Bottom Cups, 110
    Blueberry Buttermilk
        Muffins, 105
    Boston Brown-Bread
        Muffins, 112
    Brenda's Bran Muffins, 113
    Brown-Sugar Oatmeal
        Muffins, 102
    Cranberry, Walnut &
        Orange Muffins, 106
    Good Muffins, 112

Joan Pearson's Apple Muffins,
    99
Lillie's Gingerbread
    Muffins, 111
Maggie's Raspberry Muffins,
    107
Never-Fail Blueberry
    Muffins, 104
North Woods Muffins, 101
Oats & Applesauce Muffins,
    100
Orange-Chocolate Muffins,
    110, *135*
Raspberry Honey Banana
    Muffins, 103, *135*
Raspberry Streusel Muffins,
    106
Rhubarb Muffins, 109
Smoked-Turkey Muffins, 115
Special Muffins, 101
Sweet-Potato Muffins, 114
The Very, Very Best
    Blueberry Muffins, 104
Upside-Down Muffins, 108
Winter-Squash Muffins, 113
Multigrain Bread, 172
My Favorite Biscuits, 117

N

Never-Fail Blueberry
    Muffins, 104
No-Fail Flaky Pie Crust, 26
No-Fail Pie Crust, 26
North Woods Muffins, 101
Norwegian Sweet Bread, 202
Nutritious Double-Oat
    Bread, 181

O

Oats
    Anne's Oatmeal Cookies,
        71, *134*

Brown-Sugar Oatmeal Muffins, 102
Chewy Granola Bars, 95
Crunchy-Top Peach Pie, 13
Date-Filled Cookies, 86, *130*
Gramma Freda's Oatmeal Cake, 40
Grandma's Cookies, 72
Grandma's Oatmeal Bread, 166
High-Protein Honey Wheat Bread, 191
Lemon Oatmeal Cookies, 71
Nutritious Double-Oat Bread, 181
Oat Bran Rolls, *129*, 148
Oatmeal Bread, 180
Oatmeal Chocolate Cake, 45
Oatmeal Pie, 17
Oatmeal-Raisin Chocolate-Chip Cookies, 76
Oats & Applesauce Muffins, 100
Oh Henry Bars, 94
Multigrain Bread, 172
Smoked-Turkey Muffins, 115
Special Muffins, 101
Spicy Oatmeal & Chocolate-Chip Cookies, 77
Sundial Farm Anadama Bread, 195
Texas Buffalo Chips, 72
Whole-Wheat Bread, *54*, 171
Whole-Wheat & Oatmeal Bread, 179
Oh Henry Bars, 94
Old-Fashioned Hot Cross Buns, 126
Old-Order Amish Bread, 189
Oranges
Apricot Bread, 152
Cranberry, Walnut & Orange Muffins, 106
Cranberry Date-Nut Bread, 158
Cranberry-Orange Bread, 159

Greek Walnut Cakes, 36
Kiss-Me Cake, 38
Orange Cake, 33
Orange Carrot Cake, 37
Orange Nut Bread, 160
Orange Swirl Rolls, 143
Orange Zucchini Bread, 163
Orange-Chocolate Muffins, 110, *135*
Pumpkin-Orange Pie in a Walnut Crust, 18
Smoked-Turkey Muffins, 115
Stained-Glass Pie, 15

P

Parmesan Herb Bread, 207
Peaches
Crunchy-Top Peach Pie, 13
Honey Peach Pie, 14
Peaches & Cheese Cake, 34
Peanut Butter
Bean & Butter Bread, 178
Chewy Granola Bars, 95
Easy Peanut Butter Cookies, 74
Famous Peanut Butter Cookies, 74
Magic Peanut Butter Middles, 73
Oh Henry Bars, 94
Pear Pie, 14, *53*
Pecans
Apricot Pecan Bread, 185
Blonde Brownies, 96
Christmas Casserole Cookies, 88
Cranberry Date-Nut Bread, 158
Family Treasure Butterhorns, 84
Granny Smith Coffee Cake, 62
Janhagel Cookies, 87

Lemon Oatmeal Cookies, 71
Millmoss Pie (Caramel-Topped Squash Pie), 19
Pecan Fudge Pie, 24
Pecan Praline Cookies, 78
Pecan Sticky Buns, 125
Pecan Tarts, 25
Sherry's Pecan Pie, 24
Special Muffins, 101
Special-Treat Cheesecake, 35
Spicy Oatmeal & Chocolate-Chip Cookies, 77
Texas Buffalo Chips, 72
Twenty-Minute Fudge Cake, 44
Upside-Down Muffins, 108
Winter-Squash Muffins, 113
Peda Bread, *136*, 188
Persimmon Cookies, 82
Pies & Crusts
Blueberry Pie, 12
Cherry-Berry Pie, 21
Chocolate Pie, 23
Company Pie, 16, *53*
Crunchy-Top Peach Pie, 13
Fresh Coconut Pie, 20
Honey Apple Pie, 11
Honey Peach Pie, 14
Lemon Pie, 22
Millmoss Pie (Caramel-Topped Squash Pie), 19
No-Fail Flaky Pie Crust, 26
No-Fail Pie Crust, 26
Oatmeal Pie, 17
Pear Pie, 14, *53*
Pecan Fudge Pie, 24
Pecan Tarts, 25
Pie Crust, 25
Pumpkin-Orange Pie in a Walnut Crust, 18
Quantity Pie Crust, 27
Raisin Pie, 16
Rhubarb Cream Pie, 20
Sherry's Pecan Pie, 24
Spiced Rhubarb-Strawberry Pie, 21
Stained-Glass Pie, 15

Sugarless Apple Pie, 11, *56*
Sweet-Potato Pie, 17
Pistachio Icebox Cookies, 78
Poppy Seed
    Almond & Poppy-Seed
      Muffins, 99
    Poppy-Seed Bread, 154
Pound Cake, 40
Prize-Winning Applesauce
  Cake, 57
Prune Cake, 39
Pumpkin
    Choco-Dot Pumpkin Cake,
      60
    Pumpkin Cake Roll, 61
    Pumpkin-Orange Pie in a
      Walnut Crust, 18
    Sherry Pumpkin Bread, 161

Q

Quantity Pie Crust, 27
Quick Breads
    Alice's Brown Bread, 167
    Apricot Bread, 152
    Apricot-Raisin-Bran Bread,
      152
    Banana & Sour-Cream
      Bread, 153
    Buttermilk-Herb-Tomato
      Bread, 168
    Carrot Corn Bread, 169
    Carrot-Nut Bread, 160
    Cherry Bread, 156
    Chocolate Zucchini Bread,
      164
    Cranberry Bread with
      Cream Cheese, 159
    Cranberry Date-Nut Bread,
      158
    Cranberry-Orange Bread, 159
    Date-Nut Bread, 155
    Fresh Ginger Banana Bread,
      154
    Grandma's Oatmeal Bread,
      166

Grape-Nuts Bread, 165
Irish Freckle Bread, 166
Lemon Tea Bread, 156
Mexican Corn Bread, *55*, 169
Morning-Glory Bread, 157
Orange Nut Bread, 160
Orange Zucchini Bread, 163
Poppy-Seed Bread, 154
Quick Cinnamon Bread, 151
Rhubarb Bread, 162
Sherry Pumpkin Bread, 161
Squash Spoon Bread, 168
Strawberry Bread, 161
Zucchini Bread, 165

R

Raisins
    Apple-Raisin Bread Braid, 184
    Apricot-Raisin-Bran Bread,
      152
    Oatmeal-Raisin Choco-
      late-Chip Cookies, 76
    Raisin Bread, 183
    Raisin Pie, 16
Raspberries
    Black Raspberry Muffins, 108
    Cherry-Berry Pie, 21
    Maggie's Raspberry Muffins,
      107
    Raspberry Bars, 91, *133*
    Raspberry Cream-Cheese
      Coffee Cake, 67
    Raspberry Honey Banana
      Muffins, 103, *135*
    Raspberry Streusel Muffins,
      106
Refrigerator Coffee Cake, 69
Rhubarb
    Rhubarb Bread, 162
    Rhubarb Coffee Cake, 62
    Rhubarb Cream Pie, 20
    Rhubarb Muffins, 109
    Spiced Rhubarb-Strawberry
      Pie, 21
    Yummy Rhubarb Squares, 92

Rich Shortcake Biscuits, 120
Rich Yeast Rolls, 146
Rolls, *see Biscuits, Buns & Rolls*
Russian Black Bread, 199
Rye, *see also Biscuits, Buns &*
  Rolls; Muffins; Quick Breads;
  Yeast Breads
    Caraway-Rye Bread, 200
    Clara Lydell's Rye Bread, 201
    Grossmutter's Rye-Meal
      Bread, 200
    Russian Black Bread, 199

S

Sandwich Bread, 205
Savory Dill Bread, 211
Seasonal Fruitcake, 65
Sherry Pumpkin Bread, 161
Sherry's Pecan Pie, 24
Shortbread, 88
Sinbad Bars, 94, *133*
Smoked-Turkey Muffins, 115
Sour-Cream Twists, 145
Sour Dough
    Sourdough Bread I, 212
    Sourdough Bread II, 214
    Sourdough Starter, 213
Special Muffins, 101
Special-Treat Cheesecake, 35
Spiced Rhubarb-Strawberry
  Pie, 21
Spicy Oatmeal & Chocolate-
  Chip Cookies, 77
Squash, *see also Zucchini*
    Millmoss Pie (Caramel-
      Topped Squash Pie), 19
    Squash Spoon Bread, 168
    Winter-Squash Muffins, 113
Stained-Glass Pie, 15
Strawberries
    Cherry-Berry Pie, 21
    Spiced Rhubarb-Strawberry
      Pie, 21
    Strawberry Bread, 161

Sugarless Apple Pie, 11, *56*
Sundial Farm Anadama
 Bread, 195
Surprise Cookies, 80
Swedish Rolls, 140
Sweet Potatoes
 Sweet-Potato Muffins, 114
 Sweet-Potato Pie, 17

T

Texas Buffalo Chips, 72
Tweed Squares, 97
Twenty-Minute Fudge Cake, 44

U

Unconventional Fruitcake, 39
Upside-down Muffins, 108

V

The Very, Very Best Blueberry
 Muffins, 104

W

Walnuts
 Cranberry, Walnut &
  Orange Muffins, 106
 Greek Walnut Cakes, 36
 Pumpkin-Orange Pie in a
  Walnut Crust, 18
 Unconventional Fruitcake, 39
 Walnut Bread with Allspice
  Butter, 176
Whole Wheat, *see also Biscuits,*
 Buns & Rolls; Muffins; Quick
 Breads; Yeast Breads
 Whole-Wheat & Oatmeal
  Bread, 179

Whole-Wheat Bread, *54*, 171
Whole-Wheat Herb Braid,
 204
Winter-Squash Muffins, 113

Y

Yeast Breads
 Apple-Raisin Bread Braid, 184
 Apricot-Pecan Bread, 185
 Bean & Butter Bread, 178
 Beer Bread, 202
 Braided Dill Bread, 210
 Buckwheat Bread, 182
 California Squaw Bread, 173
 Caraway-Rye Bread, 200
 Cindy's Wheatberry Bread,
  192
 CJ's E-Z Herb Bread, 203
 Clara Lydell's Rye Bread, 201
 Dilly Casserole Bread, 210
 Eagles Bread, 187
 Early Colonial Bread, 196
 Everyone's Favorite Braided
  Bread, 198
 Favorite All-Purpose Bread,
  175
 French Bread, 209
 French Bread Strombolli
  Xpress, 208
 Graham-Flour Bread, 190
 Grossmutter's Rye-Meal
  Bread, 200
 Health Bread, 197
 Hearty Focaccia, 206
 High-Protein Honey Wheat
  Bread, 191
 Holiday Stollen, 215
 Italian Wheat Bread, 174
 Massachusetts Anadama
  Bread, 194
 Mike's Potato Whole-Wheat
  Bread, 177
 Mountaineer Maple Bread,
  186
 Multigrain Bread, 172
 Norwegian Sweet Bread, 202

Nutritious Double-Oat
 Bread, 181
Oatmeal Bread, 180
Old-Order Amish Bread, 189
Parmesan Herb Bread, 207
Peda Bread, *136*, 188
Raisin Bread, 183
Russian Black Bread, 199
Sandwich Bread, 205
Savory Dill Bread, 211
Sourdough Bread I, 212
Sourdough Bread II, 214
Sourdough Starter, 213
Sundial Farm Anadama
 Bread, 195
Walnut Bread with Allspice
 Butter, 176
Whole-Wheat & Oatmeal
 Bread, 179
Whole-Wheat Bread, *54*, 171
Whole-Wheat Herb Braid,
 204
Yummy Rhubarb Squares, 92

Z

Zucchini
 Chocolate Zucchini Bread,
  164
 Orange Zucchini Bread, 163
 Zucchini Bread, 165